GREATEST MISTAKE

Therefore, I encourage everyone to read it

CEE EZIAMAKA

Greatest Mistake

Copyright © 2024 by Cee Eziamaka.

Disclaimer

All rights reserved.

No parts of this publication may be produced or transmitted in any form or by any means, electronic or mechanical, including photocopy, recording or any information storage and retrieval system, without permission in writing from the publisher. Unless otherwise indicated, biblical quotations from the King James Version. All stories related in this book are true, but most of the names have changed to protect the privacy of the people mentioned.

ISBN: 978-1-917124-42-3

For information contact :
Website: https://greatestmistakesharpmindedcriminals.com/
Email: inforgreatestmistake@gmail.com

Table of Contents

Note	5
Introduction	6
Deep Seated Issues	12
Spirit's Trick	28
Mr, Reverend	51
Greatest King	93
After My Heart	116
Ultimate Secret	126
24hrs Awareness	159
Urgent Attention, Singles	176
No wed, Still	213
Spirit's Conviction	228
Readers Where Have You Affected	245
Dating Sites/ Open Marriage	279
Abraham Is Our Father	309
Spirit whispers	323
Visions, dreams and promises, spirits ways	333
Professional Liars -	342
Conclusions:	353
Apologies	357

The author says that his experience was as unpalatable as it was traumatic. He says he would hate to see even his enemies go through a similar one as a result of ignorance. Therefore, he says he encourages everyone to read it.

Edited and forwarded by

Aguoha B.O.

NOTE

I deeply appreciate my family, relatives, and in-laws who have supported me during this challenging and distressing situation. To my friends in London's scrapyards and all well-wishers who have visited and especially those who have offered encouragement, I thank you. To the ministers who have lent a helping hand in this trying time, my gratitude is boundless. I'd also like to thank the editors and publishers for their diligent work and significant contributions that brought Greatest Mistake to completion. Additionally, I must acknowledge the screenwriters for all your encouragement and support.

Above all, my heartfelt appreciation goes to my mother, Diana Eziamaka, for her surviving resilience and unwavering encouragement during my absence.

Criticisms, well, I can say we all are still learning, for we learn every day. I, in truth, love you all.

Many thanks
Cee Eziamaka

INTRODUCTION

One thing we need to understand is this—when we mention spirits, many of us do not truly grasp what these beings are. Furthermore, these beings are often given other names, which are familiar and based on certain traits and characteristics they exhibit; even though they are spirits, they behave much like humans, and because they are among the few entities that can deduce and understand human thoughts, they hold a certain influence over our minds. This book also suggests that religion began through a compelling story. I would argue that because religion became key to our survival, safeguarding these beliefs is of immense importance, often under the guise of divine inspiration. This might explain why spirits emulate traditional forms of leadership to represent the throne of the Creator.

Introduction

These volumes discuss deep-seated issues—specifically, the reasons why spirits continually deceive us. The book is supplemented with illustrations and pictures. It elaborates on how ancestral (familiar) spirits observe and fly around each one of us in the world today. In doing so, might they observe our actions and improve upon them in more effective ways?

Three-quarters of today's human problems, particularly in third-world countries, can be attributed to these beings. For instance, incidents of madness are often a result of spiritual influence. Spirits are also responsible for tragedies such as bushfires, residential fires, and market fires, which lead to significant property damage and plunge many into poverty. Furthermore, these spirits are believed to cause road accidents by luring drivers, especially those driving at night, into slumber. Issues like poverty, illiteracy, and misunderstandings among relatives and close allies can also be attributed to them. Inflicting these adversities upon humans appears to be a primary source of pleasure for these beings.

The Holy Spirit, Ancestral Spirits (Familiar), and Satan (Devil) — while these names are often used interchangeably, they have been distinguished and renamed over time due to their varied tactics and methods, primarily to sow confusion. These spirits have existed for ages, just like every other living entity. The book delves into their origins and the unique abilities they possess.

This book illuminates how naive we can be in the face of these cunning beings (familiar spirits). They've swayed our beliefs, leading us away from what we once understood. The text also explores the relationship between us and these spirits, highlighting our susceptibility to their influence. Moreover, it addresses the ways in which we have been misled regarding our core beliefs.

Many thanks,
Cee Eziamaka.

Introduction

GREATEST MISTAKE

Wow! It is a pity. Remarkable Experience: Nonentity Spirits have been making fools of the wise for millions of ages.

Therefore, I encourage everyone to read it.

This is where entire World problems declined; African countries, the most religious with millions of spiritual and self-appointed Gospel Ministers and still, these countries are in a mess.

The wickedness of the Spirits churches etc., worships our eyes, ears and mind needs awareness of the beings around us 24hrs:

Let I say it clearly, any Company in the World today that will first produce what it takes to be killing of the spirits (devils) that's monitoring human beings since all these while without affecting human's life, SKY will be their limits. Which will enable divorce marriages, nation fighting against nation, corruptions, madness, family problems, and many more will decree to almost zero, because the same spirits behind it all.

ATTENTION HERE.
SCRIPTURES:

That the whole world was once covered by floor of catastrophic proportions, and only eight persons survived (Gen: Chapters 6 and 7)

That the earth will yet be destroyed by fire (11Peter, Ch. 3 verse7 and 10)

That Noah built his Ark in 40 days.
That Rain/storm lasted for 40 days
Israelites walked through the desert for 40 days
Jesus fasted for 40 days and 40 nights.

Isaac was 40 yrs. when he married Rebecca, Abraham was 30 yrs. when having problems of conception with Sarah.

Jesus Christ was 30 yrs when he started having problems in his Ministry.
Jacob was 30 yrs., when he made a decision to settle down, in the process, started having problems with Laban.

Introduction

FURTHER

That Adam lived for 930 years and died.
Seth lived for 912 years and died.
Cain lived for 910 years and died.
Noah lived for 950 years and died.

Enoch lived for 365 years, and God took him.
Again, Elijah went up by the awhirl wind into
Heaven as recorded. Scripture further says that
because of sin, He decreased the days of Man.

These above are the Spirit's way of boasting,
as you/I can self-praise far more are these
authorities/Spirits of the entire World religions.

DEEP SEATED ISSUES

*L*et's face it, there are deep-seated issues. I would like us to understand this: when we mention the *spirits*, many of us will not understand what such beings are. Now, I would like to take the time to define the word "spirit". I will say there are two types of spirits; spirit world and spirit mind.

First, I will talk about the *spirits world*, which is well-known to man; they are initially known as Ancestral beings. Spirit world reproduces like every other living being by laying eggs in the green grasses on Earth. They can be compared in number to the sand in the desert, which is everywhere.

Moreover, these beings are also given other names, familiar spirits due to their characteristics. Even though they are spirits, they behave exactly like humans because they are the only living thing that can deduce and understand man's mind, allowing them to take control of man through religion. Also, we have accepted the being's convictions, unaware right from the Ancestors (Ancient forms of worship), and the beings, because of their wicked nature, have no option but to take control and act as regarded, which also resulted in the modern ways of religion, and by these, some sects of the faiths.

Christians, in turn, promoted the beings unaware of a job well done by baptising them with a new name called *Holy Spirit*. These are the reason scriptures say that the Creator is a spirit, and the mind/Spirit of the Creator is Holy. These are also confirmed in John 4:24. The beings that the church worship is reproduced by laying eggs in the green grass.

However, the second type of spirit is called the *spirit mind*. To define the spirit mind, I will say that we can recognise the spirit mind as something so crucial to us. This clarification will help us understand that there is no different or particular spirit inside every human. So, anybody or any scripture that says there are three Spirits in a Man; Spirit of Creator, the mind of Man, and a sacred of the Devils that leads us to Sin. These have been led astray.

Anyway, the spirit mind that you (or I) have is called the spirit mind; this is why the scripture says that Jesus is the

Spirit of the Creator. Likewise, the scripture says that the Spirit of the Creator is in us all, which means that we are his spirit. Why? Because Jesus and humans are so crucial to the Creator, according to the Scriptures. That is why he, at all times, keep the focus where we are because he claims he created Man through his image.

Another example: If I tell you that you are a spirit to your parents, I do not think I have made a mistake because if Jesus/human being is His Spirit, then you are also a Spirit to your Parents.

This is because they brought you into being; you are so precious, so valuable to them, and their spirit mind is always where you are as Jesus is to Creator. All means one can with a sound mind (God) representing your good intentions. Also, at the same time, one can have an awful account (devils), representing terrible intents. These do not mean there is a particular Spirit of them inside us.

However, you need to reason the scripture's ways and explain the Spirit of the Creator inside us.

According to the biological understanding, we believe by the conviction that the congregation of the children of Israel in the scriptures represents today's ongoing religion, spiritual Israel. However, the secret is this – many of us, the modern people in today's religions, are not aware that the intentions and plans the spirits had for the children of Israel in the wilderness is Proverbs—*a* picture of what the spirits also had in mind, in stock for present day's religions.

However, a considerable percentage of us lack this understanding. For example, the Old faiths promised a Land, which signifies Heaven promised to today's Christians/Religions. Again, the Old beliefs sinned by defiling the land in Egypt with their Idol worship, and the spirits decided to bring them out from that sin.

On the other hand, the area of promise filled with milk and honey has provided for them. On the other hand, according to the scriptures, modern people, born of a woman, have sinned through the sin of Adam and Eve. Spirits had promised through Jesus to forgive us and bring us out from our Adamic sin, and a promise of Heaven was made to them but under submission. So, note that the spirits first deceived ancient people because of the sin of their Idol worships. Then, the Arabic, the Book of

Moses, and the Old Testament were established, and the land, filled with milk and honey, was promised. They all died at the end of the journey: they did not enter. Their leader Joshua and Caleb that remains is a Spirit's adage. It symbolises the well-being of today's ministers that is still leading today's congregation for the spirits because their minds cannot do without the use of humans.

Whereas modern people were misled for the second time because of the sin of Adam and Eve. Then, by the redemption of the blood of Jesus, they have been forgiven. The sky (Heaven) promised to anyone who obeyed. The New Testament is also established. Today, as we live, we are also in the wilderness like the children of Israel. We are heading to Heaven (Hell) with the spirits through life afflictions. Along the line, many faiths died every day without getting into that heavenly promise, as the children of Israel did not either. Their families and relatives here on Earth did not know as well where they were after death.

The 'Greatest Mistake' points out that they keep misleading us; I will furnish you with an illustration: A picture of what I'm edifying, as it has been said. Spirits monitors are soaring around every one of us today. So, they were learning what we were doing and could put it into practice more effectively.

For example, my origin is from the Igbo tribe (Biafra) in Nigeria, and the Familiar Spirits monitor me twenty-four hours without option, right from my baby's age. They speak my local dialects well because they are also raised in my village. If I have acquired studying and am able to speak another language, the being's monitors do. likewise, they catch on to things faster than humans in all we do. Still, humans have a better understanding, sympathetic and compassionate. Though, they can put things into practice even in a way better than humans.

These are the grounds for interacting, monitoring, and controlling many aspects of human behaviour. Also, this is why they are called Familiar Spirits. While they were originally called Ancestral Spirits, the Satan/Devils here on Earth. Through their deception through religion, they are baptised with a new name called Holy Spirit by Christians. In understanding, they are in existence even before humans. So, they are not strangers; they are the indigene of the land. They also reproduce likewise and are in colours, black and brown like other living things and can be killed with clove oil and active fly killer because they take a breath, the worst part is they can discern/read and understand the mind of you or me.

These are their highest secret. However, mind you, they have limited power. They can only make a few things come to pass, mostly through conviction. These are the reasons the faiths are praying without season. Still, things keep on not coming as expected, and most of the words of the promises in the Scriptures are not fulfilling as regarded.

So, whatever we are doing, the beings that are Familiar to Man does it much more. However, listen carefully to this – Human's ways of using proverbs, mostly in the old days, was beautiful. I will do my very best to make the meaning very clear for us to understand. As have said somewhere in those days, Ancestors preferred proverbs, idioms for advice, correction, instruction, and rebuking, ways of righteousness, and that what the Scriptures are all about. They have been doing that due to the characteristic of Human's behaviours. So, when something takes place uncountable times, then that will be seen as a custom/tradition before the people. People will use that as a kind of reference either in Proverb or Idiom, and it continues that way. These are the reasons the human way of proverbs looks more real any time such words will be uttered, maybe in proverbs or in Idioms. If you give reason to it, you will be able to learn something out of it. So, whatever you are doing, the beings monitors do likewise and can remember the history more than Humans.

However, here are some examples. These are the main lifestyles of our ancestors. Today, due to enlightenment and developments, they seem to have been forgotten. Nevertheless, people are still living this kind of lifestyle, mostly the elders, when they are talking with the juniors, and that also helps elders understand the level of their knowledge and the use of their initiatives. It seemed like a tradition in those days, and they could do these maybe to stir the juniors up for better understanding and to the text of their initiatives. Even to the point, pupils had lessons in the schools for idioms, proverbs, and tales. They could sometimes hold it in the classrooms, under the trees, or in the playing ground, and so on. Even people in the villages usually gather in town halls or playing grounds for this folklore.

In my local dialect, it says: proverbs and Idioms are like sauce/stew. So, it was widespread in those days.

Consequently, they will be doing all these for instructions, advice, corrections, and rebuking.

Well, if you have witnessed what I'm talking about, then you will be able to understand that those tellers mostly use some of these words below:

- About snakes (Serpents)
- About tortoises
- About a king(s)
- About an elephant
- About hippopotamus
- About the king's first son or daughter
- About a Queen
- About a decree of a king and his province
- About wealth, etc.

On the other hand, after someone has given a tale talk in front of the class or a group of people, then the teacher or an elder will come up with some questions that help the questioner to determine how well and serious his pupils/people are in the class. Very common in those days, and as they were doing it, the familiar spirits were walking and monitoring everyone, now were with them, listening and learning. All they were saying and doing, without them being aware, as very many of us were not aware of the beings around us today.

Now, I will give an illustration of human ways of proverbs and Idioms.

Examples:

A proverb says a person who never dreamt of being a king later becomes a king. He will, from the ankle of his foot, wear a rope, which signifies his title. Well, it does not mean the person will put on the rope, as said, but due to the present life of that individual. It may be in good motive, and also, it may be in a lousy reason. Although, when such a thing happens, the characteristics of that person are likely to be seen as unusual.

I will use the character of some politicians, for example: Which you may have witnessed during some political campaigns. Many politicians will be saying all things they can be unable to do, with their sweet tongue, to be nominated by the masses. Also, after the campaign has been done, eventually, if elected, within a couple of months or, taking the position, his/her character will change, and, to extents, some of the party members will see ignored. These will result in many of the members that will be disfavoured. A lot of promises made during the campaign will seem impossible to fulfil. You will also witness the vehicle, the person will be using to the extent of some of the party members, will feel shy to meet with him. These types of lifestyles are to let you know how he/she is on top.

Further examples are some of our professional footballers. Those who never dreamt of being wealthy, handling good money, and when some of them are opportune of being involved as a professional footballer, as a result of big wages offered, then you will see that their character will never seem the same, and if you meet up those that run after women, you will see how they waste money. The types of cars, their private houses and the rest, you will be amazed. These couple of examples are the meaning of human ways of proverbs, as stated above.

Further Illustration:

In those days, there was a King in the land of Israel, King Joke, who reigned for many years. He was so influential in his time and very wealthy in Stock, to the extent that in his household, everything uses was of pure gold, including his house gate and the wall fence. In one of the highest hills in Israel was where he built his dwelling, and his business ships sailed to many Nations in the land of Israel. Whatever he decreed came to pass, and people submitted to his authority. It happened that the King had only one son, Zoo, by name, and a daughter. He decreed that at the end of the year, a festival would be held at his palace.

However, whenever such a feast is held, Kings and people from all tribes will come with things needed for the celebration; it was the tradition in those days, even to these days in many places, and on the day of the feast. The King decreed all people from all tribes would come up with their traditional music. Masquerades of all kinds and gifts for the festival. Because he is King of Kings, in the land of Israel,

Due to the tradition at that time, at the throne where the King was seated, people bowed down to worship the King and his image as the custom for his righteousness and holiness. Due to the culture, any time such a feast will be held; The King's son would be seated at his right hand. As you know, due to the culture and the power of a King, not likely for an outsider to see or know King's Wife in those ancient times.

Outstanding this traditional custom in the land of Israel. Any year, the King's festival will be during the celebration. The King would be making some announcement (budget) before his people, like today's presidents and prime ministers, do at the beginning of the year. The laws and decree that he uses to govern his people in the land of Israel. Anyone who walked against the King's orders and authority (commandment, like that in the bible) would be regarded as an enemy of the King's government and would face judgment before the King, according to the decree.

Examples

- » Any criminal (migrant) acts will face judgment according to the decree of the King.
- » Fornication and immoral behaviour will face trials.
- » Taking over somebody's land will be persecuted by laws.
- » Selfish behaviour will be taxed.
- » None or delayed payment of the annual levy will face trials.

» Anyone found not being obedient to the King's decrees and commandments has already become an enemy to the King.

» The King pronounces before his subjects in the Land of Israel. That they will keep on announcing or keep everyone informed (Testifying of his Kingdom, Evangelising) of all the decrees, authority, and his commandments. Similar to what today's faiths are doing.

Well, we are still on the human ways of giving stories. It so happened after years of King Joke holding power. He decided to celebrate his wealth achievements. He decrees in the land that all the animals, including human animals, will come before King Joke. Kings, Princes, and the people of all nations were quite aware that all the livings were also animals.

Moreover, the King made a decree on occasion. Invitees have to attend with a present of their choice for the celebration. Also, in those days, you need not be told, and you cannot go to a celebration party or house of a King without a present. Another solemn promise he made before the message of his Kingdom in the land of Israel

Greatest Mistake

was decreed over those presents that any Animal who will come on the day of the celebration with an elephant will be the highest quest for the ceremony. King also vowed before subjects. That an Animal will marry the King's first Daughter. The King will allow the couple to live in his palace. Also, a particular title promised to the King's in-law before the presence of all people in Israel.

Well, it happened that right from the week of celebration, all the Animals started coming from every direction for the commemoration: In essence, some Animals came with Yams, Banana, Cassava, while some came with Plantain, Mangoes, Oranges, Pears, and some other Fruits, while some Humans.

Animals came with Cola Nuts, Coconuts, Calabash, and Jars of Palm Wine. Some other Human Kings brought Female Sheep, Female Goats, and many different gifts for the celebration at the same time some of the Animals like Lions, Snakes (Bible Serpent), Tiger, and the rest managed to bring themselves to the party. The Chips (Chimpanzees) seen as the highest Animals that brought a Basket of Palm Nuts, Mangoes, and Banana to the King, to the greatest surprise of all. After all, the invitees had arrived for the occasion. There was King, seated on his

Throne, watching and waiting to see the Animal that would arrive at the celebration venue with an Elephant as pronounced.

SPIRIT'S TRICK

Then, the Tortoise was the only Animal that came last. On Tortoise': s way, he rang with the message that the Journey was too far from one end to the other. However, it will arrive shortly with the Elephant, as pronounced by The King.

So, as the Tortoise finished giving the message over the phone, the Elephant then asked him (the Tortoise) what he said. However, the Tortoise responded, "no," I was singing that the Land will continue keeping Elephants because they are too big, bigger than all the Animals. Then the Elephant said to the Tortoise "ok," so both Tortoise and Elephant continued on their way for the King's celebration. On their way, the tortoise complained bitterly to the Elephant; the journey was too long. He felt pain all over his Ankles, desperately pleaded Elephant to help have him on his back to make their ride faster.

Since the Elephant was the biggest Animal in the forest, the Elephant agreed and mellowed down, and the Tortoise climbed on its back as he (Tortoise) was seated at the back of the Elephant. He was singing a song of joy that he is recognized as the least among all Animals in the forest of Israel (the Entire World). However, today, he is the one who knows how to relate to all the Animals in the woods (Land).

When they were a few miles away before the celebration venue, the tortoise came up again with a question before the Elephant. Did he ask? "Would you agree to what I will tell you now? "The Elephant asked, "What is it?" the Tortoise said, "no," but give me **Yes** or No answer. Then the elephant said "yes" to the question. Then the tortoise said, let me get down from your back and put a rope around your neck, and I will hold the line as we are going to make our journey quicker. The elephant responded Fine; the tortoise did it that way. As they were about to arrive at the venue, the tortoise started over again singing joyful songs, telling the king that other animals big and small are afraid of the elephant. Because he is the biggest animal in the land of Israel, but I, the tortoise, the least among all the animals, have brought the elephant, the biggest of all, to you as pronounced.

Then, as Tortoise arrived with an Elephant for the ceremony, he went straight to the King, who was seated at the Throne, and handed him over the rope of the Elephant. The King commanded everyone to stand up for the Tortoise to be congratulated for the job well done because the Tortoise was the only Animal in the land who met up with the King's demand. In that ceremony, the daughter of the King handed over to the Tortoise as his husband. A house in the King's palace as promised, was presented to them too. The highest titles given to the Tortoise on occasion were each, and everyone in Israel would hear of his name (tortoise). Also, his name would be in all the stories that will be in the land of Israel. It signifies reasons. The name tortoise is always said in most of the tale's/stories people were giving in every area of Israel now and then. These are the reasons; sometimes, you may be having some issues with somebody, and out of a sudden, one person may say to the other. "Do not try to be the tortoise, or are you a tortoise?"

Then, all the invitees started complaining, saying, how did it happen? Tortoise, least of all Animals is the only Animal that brought an Elephant to the King, even the human that is with a high sense of reasoning. Is it because Tortoise seemed more cunning than every other animal in the Land of Israel.

They all started looking for the Tortoise to get killed. For these reasons, Tortoise hiding and complaining that decree was made open by the King, which all the Animals accepted/ agreed. So why did they wanted to kill him? Was it because the tortoise is the least of all the animals, and added that he is also indigent of the land that it can never be possible?

Then, on the day of the traditional marriage (White Wedding) between the Tortoise and the King's

Daughter. Many and other Kings attended. The highest miracle that happened at that time was palm wine, which they brought for the traditional marriage before the presence of the people on that occasion. King Joke added water into it, and all tasted likewise, and then the people marvelled, praising his name and nicknames. It may be available for the people and also to witness the people of

Israel. Nothing is impossible with the King. He decrees, and it came to pass, and these are the reasons; these days, if you watch closely, you will witness the wines taper. After they have brought the first wines, they add some water into it to increase the quantity, and the wine still tastes the same. After many years of the tortoise's marital life, the wife died without a child. Now, the King had only one son. Since then, the tortoise was still single, living alone, and full of humiliation. These are some reasons why Tortoise observed at all-time walking alone.

My dear, these are the examples of human ways of stories now and then, and also, this story is the pillar and the foundation of the entire history of the Entire World Religion message season.

If I ask, these days, why, Rev, Fathers, and Sisters uniquely dancing Biafra traditional Ogene music, lifting Holy hands. Devil so con?

In its real meaning;

For a better understanding of the stories regarding King Joke, an Elephant, and the Tortoise:

If I ask, according to the explanation of the stories above, has King Joke ever lied or changed his words before his subjects in the land of Israel?

Well, even if he did, but due to the tradition in the land of Israel. There is never a time; a name will say to a traditional King that he lies over an issue. However, they can only address him with a word of the proverb by looking thoroughly at these issues and check it yourself. Similar to what scripture says that the Creator cannot lie or take back/change the words that come/proceeded out of his mouth.

According to the scripture, these are also the reasons the faiths believed the Creator, the King, cannot lie or change his Words?

Now and then, what is the real meaning of a King in the tale language?

Look, in tale language, the name King Means God of/before his subjects.

Further, if I want to define the name King today, it all means somebody who is a ruler that has domain and Kingdom: Who stands in the higher authorities.

Maybe, ruler of the world as we accepted and believed by convictions of the spirits that there is a Creator. Who rules and governs us, and we are his people, and he is our ruler, King, and our Lord. Also, maybe in a nation, in a society, or even in a town, if you do not mind, these are the reasons it said in the scripture (Psalm10:16) "The Lord is King forever and ever. The Nations have perished out of His Hand," please give this a reason, the Scripture says in (Revelation19:16) "And he has a robe on his thigh, a name written: King of Kings and Lord of Lords" (Isaiah 9:6) says, "The government shall be upon his shoulder."

Who was King Joke in the Land of Israel, and does kingship remains in their family now?

King Joke, in the land of Israel, is like God, the King of Israel, Jesus, the King of Israel, etc., but mind you, it's all stories. Because no one in particular in the Land of Israel is known as King Joke, for the same thing applies to any sects of religion in the world today, believing in any spirits regarded as the Creator, The King in the land of Israelis. Then why is no exact place to be identified within the land of Israel (world). People of this age are not able to see their family roots/records. Mind you that this also applies to all the names of the Kings written in any religious bibles.

Why and what is the reason for the King's son sitting at the right hand of the Father?

Well, I can say it is the manner. Son sitting at the right hand of the Father is never a surprise to the subjects because, according to tradition, the first son, at any given time takes over the throne of his Father after he has died.

Therefore, when the son is growing up, he has to learn things the Father is doing in case the King is seen no more because of its culture, modern civilization, even until these days, also, a lot of Tribes now doing that by rotation as mentioned. So, the King's son will be seated in a golden chair with all kinds of robes similar to what the Father is wearing. Also, this is the reason the scriptures addressed us to understand that after

Jesus had delivered the message of his Father's kingdom, he went back and occupied his seat at the right hand of the Father.

Who is the Tortoise that deceived the Elephant? The biggest of all Animals in the Land of Israel and brought him before the King.

That's a big question, but if you are familiar with the language of the tale, then you will not find it difficult. Well, I will do my best to make it very clear for us to understand.

In the language of tales, a tortoise represents anything whose movement and appearance are not straight before humans. So, in this tale, the tortoise represents the spirits (Devils, Ancestral/Familiar) spirits, which are also the Serpents/Snake that deceived Adam and Eve in the bible.

These are the three things seen very cunning in the language of tales before men. The text says in the book of (revelation12:9), "So the great dragon cast out that serpent of old, called the Devil and Satan who deceives the whole world."

"Like a roaring lion and a charging bear is the wicked ruler over the poor people. (Congregations) (Proverbs28:15). Well, give it a reason (1Peter5:8)" Be sober and be vigilant because of your adversary the devils that walk about like a roaring lion seeking whom he may devour. Also, I hope you still remember the explanation about how the serpent (snake) is written in the stories of Adam and Eve. So, these are the three things that are seen as very cunning before men in the language of tales. So, in conclusion, the Tortoise that deceived/convinced the elephant (man) is the natural ancestral/familiar spirit being and brought the elephant (man/unbeliever) to the house (Church) of the King (Creator), for worship.

What does it mean, in tale language, seating down of a King in his throne? It all means so powerful. These were the reasons the spirits imitated that ancient day's traditional way of leadership. To picture, the Throne of Creator in Heaven, seated, while the Earth is his footstool for his inhabitants.

How did you reason this? That the elephant (man) brought before the King (Creator) and his subjects by the tortoise (spirits)?

Well, in its meaning, the elephant (human) represents today's unbelievers (Disobedient people). Before the commandment of the King/Minister. So now, as tortoise (familiar spirits/evangelist) witness to him about the requirement of the king/Creator and was convinced, believed, and repented. Then, they brought the man to the house/church of the King/Creator for fellowship/worships. The scripture says that if you believe, then based on this, it will happen to you. King Abraham (a minister) believed Him, and it was accounted for him righteous.

What are the reasons that move Tortoise straight to the Throne, where the King was seated before his subjects and handed him over the rope of an Elephant (man)?

Probably, this is what is happening today in the churches. After a soul winner went out for evangelism on behalf of the church authorities and came back with a new convert, he/she goes straight to the Throne, where the King/Minister is seated before the Congregation and presents/introduces the new convert. Before the King or the Minister of the gospels for congratulation.

Why did the King ask his subjects to stand up, to congratulate the Tortoise for a job well done?

That's what happens likewise in the Churches today — after a Soul Winner has gone out for Evangelism, he came back with a new convert. Now, after a believer has introduced his disciple before the King/Minister. Then, a Minister will have no option than to ask his congregation/

flock to stand up to welcome the new convert. Also, to thank the soul winner for encouragement.

Why did the tortoise (Spirit) want yes or no answer from the Elephant (Man) before given him the reason? Here is an example of what I have said. That Tortoise represents three things, Satan/Devil, Ancestral/Familiar Spirits, and the Bible Serpent/Snake. These are the three things seen very cunning in tale language. Also, as the evangelist found the Elephant (Man, an unbeliever) then before he could be able to testify/witness to him/her the things, the requirement of the King (God). That made the Tortoise, the Evangelist, to first ask him if he believes or not. Now, the Elephant (unbeliever) responded, "Yes'. That allows the Tortoise/Familiar Spirits to start whispering/ministering him about the things, requirement, or about going to the Church/House of Creator for fellowship/worships. These also help us to understand that before the spirit/tortoise will deceive or use anybody. There must be an agreement in between. So, in conclusion, all today's ministers of the gospels, right from Pope down to the Church member, have said "yes" and accepted to the convictions of the Tortoise/Spirits before the deception takes place. Scripture words say, "If you can have believed, based on that you receive."

Now and then in tale language, what does it mean for all the animals coming out from every direction. For the celebration power of the King?

Well, as the word King represents God before his subjects, the celebration power of the King Also means church services and church activities. So, the animals coming out from every direction represent the faiths/worshippers that were going to the church – house of the King, from various houses.

Why did King Joke pronounce anyone who comes on the day of the celebration with an Elephant will be the highest guest of honour and will receive particular titles?

As the word King represents God before his people, the pronunciation/decree of King Joke, to the Elephants (The unbelievers) is similar to what the bible Creator/spirits did in the bible. He has messages of his Kingdom for his inhabitants and gives it (letter) to Jesus to go and deliver (Hebrew12:2) says, who for the joy set before him, endeavour cross, despising the shame and now has sat down at the right hand of Throne. As the Father promised

Spirit's Trick

him before bringing the message to his inhabitant. For this, Jesus said to Him, "Father, I have delivered the message you gave to me." That's why today's Ministers of the gospels frequently reminding the flocks that Jesus will be coming back soon for another message.

Throughout the reign of the King Joke, on how many occasions has he ever healed or commanded sickness to leave his subjects?

Well, one thing we need to realize is that in the tale, no particular individual in the Land of Israel is recognized/known by the name King Joke. Nevertheless, these also apply to any name written in any religious bibles, etc. As a result, right from the Bible Creator, down to the least of the Faith written in any Scripture. These are the reasons for all stories of the Spirits, whose work is defined as stealing, kill, and destroy. Which has nothing good to give to anybody, and as a result? Anybody who says to you that he/she was prayed for and healed, ignore the person and have your way out. That the person did not know what he/she encountered, and I hope you know that people make up testimonies for pride and self-esteem. These are the reasons that made some of the faith. If they're unwell, sometimes the patient will be admitted to the hospital with a bunch of Bibles at his/her bedside. After they have received treatments and gotten well, then the next thing some of them do is to appear before the congregation for testimony that the Creator has healed/saved him/her.

As mentioned above, why is it that people are not saying or hearing of the King's son?

Well, not really, but because, due to the customs, it's not that the King's subjects are unaware of the son, but mostly within the King's relatives. It is also because his Father is still active. For example, like sometimes, mature Christians will say before Abraham, Jesus was. Means, the name of Abraham is more recognized than the name of Jesus in the Ancient time. No one talks of Jesus in those days. Even though he exists in Heaven, let's assume because his Father is still active like in our Families.

As we were born, growing, and as our parents are still alive, our relatives recognize every little kid within our Family. So, the son of King Joke can only be known by his subjects when his time comes, when the father will be no more. That allows his Son to be recognized appropriately by them flogs.

Spirit's Trick

What are the reasons that permit them to monitor each and everyone in the Entire World?

Well, to answer this question, I have many reasons in my understanding of the Spirits after Wilderness on where I discovered their tricks.

The reason for monitoring everyone all this while is nature. So the spirits by origin, had the life of envy against humans. It says in many verses in the Scriptures that this authority is the Spirit of jealousy. Thus, the fact is that envy is in the bloodline of the beings, and if I want to define the word resentment, I will say it is out of wickedness. One thing is, do you know, if the envy of humans can be up to one percent, then the bitterness of these beings against humanity will be worth 99per cent? What I'm trying to say is human ways of envy are nothing compared to that of these authorities. Also, do not forget that beings envy humans because it is like humans are the only opposition they have here on Earth. If not, the Spirits should have been the next in command in all the animals because they are the following living things. Their sense is compared with that of Humans.

That's why they were not happy with the man, and coupled with they are capable of reading the mind of Man and understanding it. While no human being can understand what other people or animals have in their mind, it's only the Familiar Spirits who understand

Man's mind. Again, I do hope you're not a kid in what envy is all about.

Okay, let's look in a polygamous family where two or three women are married to one Man. You can see that in such a family, envy is already at their doorsteps knocking to be welcome.

In such a situation, if eventually, those women start to envy one another. They will likely be monitoring one another's movement in every given case. To witness an idea of what the other person is doing, whether in a good sense or bad. Even by examining all this, you find out it is all a waste of time. So, if Humans can envy their fellow Humans, then how much more, the beings that are Familiar to man, whose nature is envy. Its what life is all about.

At the same time, they are capable of reading a man's mind and understand it. Which means making fools of the humans twenty-four hours a day, including Ministers of the gospels, most with certificates: Who are in a better position to know what the beings are, are still without the real knowledge of them. That has resulted in the field of bondage for ages.

What made the elephant (humans) mellow down to enable the tortoise (the beings) to climb on his back?

The Elephant (Man) did that because of the enticing (conviction) words of the Tortoise (the Spirit). Without that, the Tortoise would not have been able to, because the Elephant is too big. Again, the other way round, without the conviction from the Tortoise. The Elephant would not have been convinced by the Tortoise because Elephants (Man) are more sensible than the Tortoise. Though Humans are really out of mind, which resulted in a great mistake, an error is part of the Animal. These paragraphs also supposed to teach us a lot in our individual lives. Because we are full of mistakes, it now results in a lot of damage here on Earth. Cause by the enemy of progress, monitoring every one of us all day. I mean, when people realize what the spirit world has done in our lives and the world at large. Then, humans will plan on how to tackle the familiar spirits because they are in our midst right here on earth.

What did you understand for the tortoise to climb on the back of an Elephant (Man)?

Well, this response may sound unbelievable, yet it is true, and we all have understood that in any tale stories, the tortoise signifies spirit, which is the bible serpent. So, do not allow this to leave your mind. From now on, those desperate ones. Who reads and understands the inner thoughts of you and I are the ones called Satan; very brutal/while in their operation as little as they are and were at every given second at the back of your body, very vigilant without option, and mostly at the back of your neck. I do not know if you understand what it means. Listening to understands what you are thinking in your mind through your echo. While other ones called the devils, are in some parts of your body attentively. Reason these, the scripture says, your body is the temple (living place of spirits), some are flying and monitoring you around. So in conclusion, these are the ideas the Tortoise asked the Elephant to mellow down and have him on his back. Life is full of wonders, I mean, when people realize what the Familiar spirits have done in our lives, and then the advanced Countries will not have an option than to tackle and wipe them out to diminish the world's problems.

Are we sure that the Tortoise married the King's Daughter for many years and later died without a Child?

Oh, yes, of course. You may now say how could this happen. There is a lot to gather from these paragraphs. I do not know if you still remember the thoughts about the Spiritual Husband. Okay, I'm here again to tell you that what is right for you and me is also good for the Spirits. Whatever man is enjoying here on Earth, the Familiar Spirits do likewise. Again, these also help us understand that the Tortoise and the King's daughter were in marital life for years without a child. Which also signifies that there will never be a time a Tortoise (Spirits can make human being conceive of giving birth to somebody). Even the other way around, it will never be possible for a human to make any Animal conceive. I think we have enough sense to know this.

It exposes self-praise stories regarding the conception of Jesus Christ through Mary by the power of the Holy Ghost. As the book of Luke has said, "So, take note that there has never been anybody like Jesus here on earth before. "That the name Jesus is stories, representing the Ancient time's first Son of the King, who succeeded his Father according to the traditional customs in the Land of Israel (World).

What and why was the Tortoise rejoicing? What made him sing joyful songs on his way to the King's festivals?

Yes, indeed, all the Tortoises in the land were happy, rejoicing with songs in their natural languages. For being able to convince the biggest Animal (Humans), which other Animals were afraid. As little as they are, they brought the Elephant before the King (Creator) of Israel (Entire World). That the ancestral (familiar) or

Holy Ghost by baptism was very happy for deceiving Human by making us believe that there is a Creator.

The King of all Kings, who rules over us, which resulted by using people to set up religions with different kinds of names here and there in every corner of the World. These are why every house of beliefs today preaches and teaches about the power of the King's (Creator) commandment (decree) and his authority. So, while the faiths are going to various Churches, Familiar Spirits walking around with every one of us will be rejoicing over the faiths (Religions) for making a fool of us because it's all tales (folklore) from the natural Ancestral Spirits, which can read and understands the inner thoughts of Man.

If I ask, what did you understand by the title given to the Tortoise (Spirits) by the King that everyone will be hearing of him in the land of Israel?

Yes, a great Title of Honour was given to the Tortoise in the land of Israel. This is similar to Titles given to Jesus, according to the Scripture, after he had delivered the message of his Father's Kingdom. It is seen as unbelievable to all the Animals that what seemed to be the least of all the Animals. The Tortoise, which every other Animal does not recognize, is the only Animals in the land that brought the Elephant to the King's events as decreed by the King. For this, after the Elephant (unbeliever) had been given to the King, before his subjects by the Tortoise.

The King also fulfilled the promise of the Title ship to the Tortoise. Now all the Animals (Humans) got attention, and they started saying several things against the Tortoise. For this, the name of Tortoise was made known to all the Animals in the land of Israel. Like, the name of Jesus is well known to all living. That what seemed to be the least of all the Animals in the Land brought the Elephant to the King's events (House of Creator, Church activities).

In all the stories mentioned above, why is it that the King's wife and daughter's names are not mentioned?

MR, REVEREND

As explained according to tradition, Women were not allowed to stand tall before Men in those days. These are the reasons why you can see mostly Male names in the Bible's Scriptures. Like in the book of (1-king and 2-kings) and also in the stories of the Children of Israel during their wilderness. You will be able to see that throughout their journey, Women were not mentioned, but not that women were not among them but were not allowed to talk verbally before Men due to culture. Which is scriptural in the book (Corinthians14:34) that says, let your women keep silent in the Church for they are not permitted to speak, but to be submissive as the laws also say. Another example I will give that will help us realize that it is all stories.

Let us cast our mind back to these that God had his only son Jesus without a daughter through Mary. Allah had only Mohammed through Amine (Amine), etc. So, the spirits heading the Religions mentioned had only one, one Male Child, the Female, was not openly said. All these are mentioned because the authorities imitated Ancient traditional ways of life and leadership to bring into being the Bibles.

A further example from the scriptures, right from the first Man and the first Woman, Adam and Eve, according to the Scriptures, had their Males Cain and Abel. Abraham and Hagar had just one Child, Ishmael.

Again, Abraham and Sarah had only Isaac. Isaac had Esau and Jacob. Then Jacob had six Male Children with Leah without a daughter. I also had Joseph through Rachel and so on. Listen to this, in the folklore; it is challenging to mention that a King had his first Child as a Female. Not in the Land of Israel.

Okay. Now, what happened to all the Kings, as stated in the volumes and the Bible. I mean, King Joke, King Nebuchadnezzar, King David, son of Jesse, King

Solomon, and all the rest of the Kings, which enables the next person after them to take over the throne?

In reality, King Zoo succeeded Father King Joke because the Father passed away, and then his son had no choice but to acquire the Father's seat. For example, this is the traditional customs in Israel. King Belshazzar succeeded the Throne of Babylon because King Nebuchadnezzar was no more. Also, King Solomon took over the Throne from his Father David in the Land of Israel, after King David had passed on and likewise other Kings in other Religious Bibles.

However, what then do you think happened to the King of Kings and the Lord of Lords (the Father, the Creator of Man) as recorded in the Bible? That seems to be Jesus taking over the Throne because the names of Jesus are mentioned everywhere in the world today?

I can say that what happened to King Joke, King Nebuchadnezzar, King David, and King Solomon was also the same thing that happened to God – that made Jesus succeed and take over the Throne, which authorized Jesus to be answering his Father's name? The Bible says Jesus Christ is God, and likewise, like many of us today, our Earthly Fathers have passed on. We then take the position of answering their names. However, let's assume that He had not passed on in life and that he had been Ancient, which made him sit down on his Throne in Heaven. While his only son Jesus is now taking care of his inhabitants

Nevertheless, to me, I don't think it is enough to get someone convinced. Because, in a sense, how will the Creator be involved in facing old age and death like ordinary humans because he is all-powerful? Though nobody will convince me that Jesus took over the Throne from his Father because his Father is Ancient. Let's look at the life of the Pope in the Catholic Church.

No matter the kind of sickness or old age that will authorities the next person to step on the Throne of the Pope to take over the position from the active Pope. That is not in the history of the Catholic Church. Or even in the human's Royal Families. So if it's not stories, then the only thing that will take a King out from the Throne is death. That has been the tradition and is also now. Nevertheless, the truth is now clear.

Why did the entire human animal in the land of Israel looking for the tortoise to kill? What did the Tortoise respond when he heard about it? All the Animals (the Entire World) were looking for the Tortoise (the familiar spirits) to kill. Animal asked a question, why was what seems to be the least of the Animals brought the Elephant (man) to the King? They wondered how it managed to happen. Humans felt the Tortoise (Ancestral Familiar) Spirits would kill for being too cunning. From that day on, all of the Animals were looking for the Tortoise (spirit world) in every direction.

When the Tortoise heard it, right from that day till now, he was hiding from the view of other Animals in the Land of Israel, with fear that they were looking for him to kill. They ask why? Was it because the Tortoise is of the least of the Animals in the Bush Garden.

The Tortoise vowed that the Land of Israel would never stand that. That Tortoise did not own any Animal; that Tortoise has a clean record in all of Israel. Also, headed that the King's decree was open for all the Animals. Luckily for the Tortoise, he succeeded over the Elephant (Man) as the King pronounced that the land of Israel helped him bring the Elephant (Humans) before the King of

Israel and before all the animals in the land of Israel. For this, animals in the land envying and gossiping about the Tortoise and Tortoise heard about it and said. No matter what one saying against the Tortoise. It will surely be in vain, and for the fact that Tortoises are also parts of the land like every other Animal, they shall not be moved.

What do you understand by ancient King Joke, adding some water into the palm-wine, before all the people in the land of Israel and it all tested likewise?

Oh, yes, though he did. It was the only way to demonstrate his power before subjects. That seems to be the lifestyle of people in power mostly. Jesus's scriptures say "On the third day, was a wedding in Canaan of Galilee, Mother of Jesus was there." now both Jesus and his disciples were invited to the wedding.

When they ran out of wine, the Mother of Jesus said to him, "They have no wine." Jesus said to her, "Woman, what does your concern have to do with me? My hour has not come." His mother said to the servants, "Whatever he says to you, do it." Now, there were set of six water pots of stones, according to the manners of purification of Jews, containing twenty or thirty gallons of apiece. Jesus said to them, "Fill the water pots with water, and they filled it up to the brim." Then he said to them, "Draw some out now and take it to the master of the feast, and they took it."

When the master of the feast tasted the water that made wine, he did not know from where it came about. However, the actions of supremacy do not mean that they made the palm-wine originally. The palm wine is natural; even up to these days, wine tapers add some water into a fresh palm wine to increase the quantity and make it more available. It still tests likewise.

Above all, what are the rewards for all the Animals that have been going for the King's feast? With all kinds of gifts and presents in the land of Israel. What profit/rewards do they get?

One of the essential things in life is awareness - coupled with having understanding, because when someone did not know where he started. May also not be able to understand where he/she ended up.

Anyway, in the language of tales above, if you're familiar, then you will be able to understand that there is nothing like rewards from King Joke or any Ancients Kings. For these, after the King's festivals have ended. All the animals (the faiths or his subjects) will depart as usual to their various houses while keeping faith and hoping that the King can protect them from the attacks of their enemies (evil people/devils).

Just similar to what is going on now and then in the churches. Because church houses are also the house of the King, where all the Humans' Animals gather for feasts/activities of the King, people attend Worship, with gifts and presents, to the Kings, and at the end of events, all depart to various houses. While keeping faith for his supremacy over lives as believers.

So, you can now see that in all things — have faith in the King because of that great promise of Heaven from the King, before the religion. You can now see that everything in the house of the King of Israel.

Is bring this and bring that, give. It shall be given back unto you, while the human animals are doing these, that animal will be going down and getting closer to old age, and these are the cause high percentage in any church today are broke. These are also the reason it is written in the scriptures, as a roaring lion and a charging bear are the wicked rulers over the poor people?

If I ask, will having religions everywhere in the world today and hearing the words, to help us be at peace or to live/abide by the Government's laws?

In these very passages, I would like to say that we have many things to iron out. Meanwhile, in these two issues, I will do my very best to expose each one in the way I look at it. Firstly, having Churches everywhere for people to attend services for the words of the Scriptures. Also, Governments should increase and stick to their laws. I will say that we all have witnessed the value of the type of spirits in our midst.

Also, the works that define their jobs are stolen, killed, and destroyed. Again, we have seen that the written words do not wholeheartedly change people from what they are and from what they are into. These contributed to Ministers of the gospels not having a fear of the bible Creator in what they are doing in the Ministry. Or, for these reasons, the Creator is not physically present with anybody.

Let's look at some third world countries that were recognized with religion and if you look around these countries, I mean, the characters of the societies, while the churches are almost in all corners of the streets. Also,

I do know that you too understand that we, the modern people mostly, go to various churches to hear the words. Also, at the same time, we are also behind whatever wrong going on in our countries. To the point, you will be surprised to see a Minister of the gospel from a third-world country in the Western World being involved in a contract marriage. Driving without comprehensive insurance coverage and driving without road tax, living in a house, and ignoring the electricity bill and television license, etc., let alone others.

So, if every Government, mostly in the third World countries, will be able to stick to its law. If anyone breaks or walk against it, then the person will receive the punishment without compromise. I mean, where the law will not have respect for anybody. Look at some countries in the western world; they are not queuing up in the Churches.

Why? Because they have respect for the law. Living by the law of their country, and their Government has no choice but to protect them through the rules. However, in some third world countries, you may even find preachers using any corner of their house to set a church without minding the outcome. People are not putting what they have heard into practice. However, when you and I abide by the laws of the Government, peace, and securities will reflect.

Sorry, for hearing that God, Jesus never existed, and these are stories, depicting the beings, and that is what was mentioned in the bible book of (Revelation12:9,). So all the Kings you see in the bible have been the ways Human beings have been living their lives here on Earth, imitated by the beings that are familiar to Man for deception.

However, since the Spirits are deceiving us, and they are right here on Earth with us. These are the reasons these beings are monitoring all the people in the Entire World today whether religious or not, they watch you, and they are always around, acting in two ways, especially to the faiths.

That means they are representing God in all good deeds, and at the same time representing the Devils in all evil acts caused by them. They will find a way to let the person concerned know by their enticing words. It is of the devil, while they are the beings behind it all. It is how they have been operating since the history of the living. Also, not that all the people written in any religious bible have existed before. Also, these are the reason that all that written in the scriptures cannot be found with today's family root. However, we lack understanding while keeping in mind that all have existed before. These are the reasons nothing is happening in any church etc., accept the miracle of conviction.

Somebody may now say, oh, "Why did it happen this way without people discovering it since all this while?"

Some Reasons Are These:

The Holy Spirit (God), Ancestral Spirits (familiar), Satan (devils)—these names are one. However, due to their tricks, ways of doing things, all sorts of names are given just for creating confusion. They have been in existence here on Earth just like every other living thing. Without proper recognition of their roots by the Ancestors, not to talk or to give appropriate notes of what they are able doing.

Lastly, in these paragraphs, if you have witnessed a good story teller or a comedian sharing stories. You will see that the teller is likely, to extend the story to any level of his/her wishes. The listeners will not find out what he/she is doing because they have already believed for the first time. Hence, after the Spirits have dealt with the Ancestors through Idol worshipping and they did not find out the Spirit's tricks. Then, the beings had no choice. Then, to substitute it to the Arabic language (the bible book of Moses). Also, the Old Testament bible of the modern religion because they have seen civilization coming to the people of this age.

However, in the process, the beings succeeded by putting all the words right from the book of Moses (Koran) into the Bible Old Testament. With the reasons that the Children of Israel had sinned against the Spirit (Creator) through their Idol worship, and the Ancestors concerned didn't find out the tricks of the beings, and they believed, accepted, and followed it up with their Children and great-grandchildren in worshipping these authorities. Then in the process, the Bible's New Testament is joined with the reason that Adam and Eve had sinned in the Garden. For these, the scriptures say all humans had sinned against the King the second time. Also, the son (Jesus) of the King, who already existed in Heaven, came in the form of Man through Joseph and Mary's Family to redeem us from our sins.

So, as the people had initially believed, then the New Testament bible was also joined and accepted by the King's subjects. You can see that in this story, the storyteller is a professional; because of this, all that is written in the New Testament Bible seems to be watered down as compared to that of scriptures in the Old Testament bible. For these reasons, beings have seen civilization coming to the subjects. Consequently, they succeeded with Arabic, the bible book of Moses, and the Old and New Testament Bibles. Then, they provided more ways of expanding the stories of the King and His Families in the bible book of Revelation. To bring in the five Testament bibles.

In these stories, it said that Jesus has to live with his people (The Righteous ones) in the next generation, which will be called New Jerusalem for one thousand years. Then, after the rapture, and by this time, Satan will bind for one thousand years. Then after, Satan will be out again to carry on with his work (deceitful ways) all over again.

As a result, you do not expect the New Jerusalem that will live with Him for the next one thousand years to use the Old and the New Testament bibles for worship. Therefore, the six guides must be provided because you can see right from my explanations of these and right from the traditional ways of worshipping. That any time He (God/Spirits) made a great promise to the subjects, the commandments, the diagrams, the decrees, the constitutions, the requirements, and the ways of worship will change. These authorities operate by giving fresh promises and new stories to the subjects, and once it did, the forms of worshipping will never be the same, and it does not end there. Again, after Jesus will be with the righteous as recorded in Revelation for 1000 years. Satan will be released; you will not also expect these authorities to continue leading the New Jerusalem (New Congregation) that will be with Him after Satan goes back to his prison yard all over again. The beings we are talking about are beings of strategies with a Ph.D. certificate in the business field of tales, tricks, and manipulations.

We are still on the message, as I understood by the Spirit acts—that whatever the beings see or hear humans do or say according to (Numbers14:28) is what they capitalize on, deceiving us (Revelation12:9). Because of this, no doubt about it that these are the exact tale talks that they use for religious deception. This is because these stories are widespread in the language of tales. If you're familiar with tales, you will be able to know that in all the tales we use, very many of it is with the title stories of Kings or Queen. Means, God in Tale stories, and if you are in the faith, you will see that all the scriptures are full of the stories of Kings and Queens, which every country and town has. However, due to civilization, too many people have stopped the traditional ways. In every Royal Family today, they had Kings/Prince and Queens, and if the present King or Queen died, then the next in line would succeed him/her, which was never a surprise to the subjects because of tradition. However, today, some countries are doing it by election or rotation. Also, some states and towns are still holding on to the old ways of doing it.

More Attention Here!

One thing I would like to remind us in these stories above, many people are used to the stories. This means, it is very common to the people exposed to stories. So what you should remember about tales is as stated above. It may not be or sound exactly like the tale you know, yet it happened.

That is the reason it is called tales. One needs to initiate very well. For example, we may be up to three or four people who understand the story about King Joke and the tortoise in the land of Israel, if the need arose for us to give this particular tale individually to a group of people. You will find out that after all of us have finished giving it, never will all of us be able to interpret or narrate it the same way. There must be differences in Interpretations, but that will also make it not to remain tales.

Again, no matter how many people contribute to the stories, at least one person must have gotten it exactly the way it needs to be. These are the reasons the names of people in the Bible interpreted the Stories of Creator (The King). In different ways, these are also the reasons you see that Matthew, Mark, Luke, John the Baptist, and Paul taught about the stories of God and Jesus, yet you find out that John's way of interpretation of God is more transparent than any other in the scriptures.

However, that does not stop others telling it in their way of understanding, while Apostle Paul narrated everything about Jesus more than any other in the Bible epistles. At the same time, it does not stop others from interpreting it in their way of understanding. Also, this is what happened to Peter, who was the disciples who understood Jesus more than any other. While Luke did exceedingly well. By the way, he narrated things concerning Mary's birth of Jesus. However, mind you, that did not also stop Mark from talking about the birth of Jesus too.

So, these are the reasons you see different names of people talking about a particular person or thing in the scriptures.

Like the way the stories of King Abraham were explained in different chapters of the bible's Old Testament and also mentioned in various sections in the New Testament. Likewise, the story of King David is also narrated in many episodes, both in the Old and New Testament. The same occurs with the stories of

Mary and how she gave birth to Jesus. Luke taught about it, Mark did, and they also mentioned in the Old Testament.

Another example of what I'm saying is this, in preaching and teaching of today's Ministers of gospels, about the Kingdom. You will see that some Ministers are very good at preaching about the stories in the Old Testament, while some are very good at teaching about the words in the New Testament.

However, at the same time, it does not stop them from talking about the words in the Old Testament, even if they are not very good at that. It all resulted in a reason, each one talking about a particular King (Creator) and his family, according to the understanding of the stories.

Remember, even though as the bible scriptures are written with different names, they adjust because it is the way, the attitude of human beings, especially the Ancestors, and their ideas of giving tales and talks in those days. In school – class by class, then, in towns, group by group. Also, this is the way today's Ministers of the gospels were standing before different sections of congregation preaching and teaching to them in the churches, etc. About the stories of the Bible King and His Family, with all kinds of manners. Again, in that manner, the beings use by ministering to them the things of the King, these authorities/spirits based on individual thinking whispers.

So, that does not mean that those names written in the bible chapters were all involved in putting down the words in any bible. The familiar spirits that inspired the writers imitated human ways of giving tales in those days just for more attention so that the people would be amazed. However, in understanding, the writing of the bible was done by one or two different Ministers through the Spirit's vision and dream instructions. As they succeeded in bringing out the Arabic, the book of Moses, and the Old Testament bible, and from these, the bible's New Testament came into being. Also, today, if modern people are still unaware, these authorities will also extend it to the 6/7 sets by using one of today's Ministers because they have already made the way in the bible Revelation, which talked about the second coming of Jesus, which will enable him to be with the righteous for one thousand years as recorded. Where life and death will be no more, while Satan and his agents will be in prison until the one thousand years are over.

However, as these authority's tricks are discovered, do not worry about where you belong on the day of the rapture. Whether On the side of Faiths (Heaven) or the bottom of the Satan (Hell). For now, all the living is currently free because we have discovered that it's all Spirit's folklores before the Entire World (Religions).

So, my dear, this is the attitude and the manner the beings that are familiar to us played. By using it, to first deceives the Ancestors that there is a Creator. The most King is Holy and is in the Sky (Heaven) seated on his Throne. Now, Idol not know? If you have witnessed the Ancient tradition. Anytime the King dies, the King's first son would take over from his Father as the customs. The Prince's taking over of the Throne is usually not a surprise to the subjects because even while his Father was alive, they accorded and praised him like his Father, the King.

Attention here:

Hope you know that all the prayers of the believers, the faiths have been praying to their Creator, which they believed lived in the sky (Heaven)? Sometimes, people will go on their knees, and some may decide to stand up, a picture, in the Ancient times, when someone or a group of people went to the King's palace, whether they saw the King or not, they would keep faith and wait until they can see the King and eventually when the King comes out; the people would be greeting the King with all manner of praises while some either kneeling or bowing to the King or may even lying down until the King asks them to stand or show a sign of respond.

That was a sign of honour to the King. They do that mostly when they want to show appreciation to the king or when they encounter problems and also when they want a favour from him. Remember the stories of King Nebuchadnezzar in the scriptures concerning Meshach, Shadrach, and Abednego.

Here are the fundamental issues, the natural beings that are familiar to man imitated the Olden days' traditional ways of life and leadership. They made it up, first, deceiving Ancestors, that there is a King of Kings in the Sky (Heaven). Whose authorities cannot be challenged. The traditional customs of honouring the King or the Royal Family in Ancient times, even up to these days in some countries, are the same way that the faiths go to churches, mosques etc. To honour what they regarded as the Creator.

Again, all the praises, thanksgiving, and all adorations given to Him are because the faiths believed He is Holy. The same occurs with the traditional King; He also receives the same because his people also regard him as someone who is Holy — Jesus Christ, sitting down at the right hand of his Father in the Throne in Heaven, as recorded. Represents/signifies the young man who is sitting beside the traditional King and learning all the things the King is doing. The scripture in (John5:19) Says, then Jesus, answered and said to them, most assuredly, I say to you, the Son can do nothing by himself, but what He sees the Father do. For whatever the Father does, the Son also does in the same manner (Verse: 20).

For the Father loves the Son and shows him all the things that he does, and he will show him more excellent works than these that you may marvel. (Verse: 22). For the Father Judges, no one but has committed all judgment to the son. (Verse: 23). That all should honour the Son, just as they honour the Father; he who does not accept the Son does not honour the Father, who sent him. (Verse: 27) And has given him the key to carry out Judgment.

Also, because he is the son, meditate on the above scriptures with respect to the ancient king's first son, as mentioned. So brethren, as Jesus is seated at the right hand of the Father as the scriptures said, and every authority has been given to him. So, like the Father (king) seen to be no more, and Jesus, the servant and the first son of the king, have succeeded him. Mind you, the same thing applies to all other religions. They all believed in worshipping different spirits without the understanding that ancestral spirits were behind it all. They existed like every other living thing and are right here on earth with us. Likewise, if the traditional king dies today, nobody will see him anymore, but only his spirits will remain. This means, his son, like Jesus, so Jesus is now answering his father's name, which is God. The scripture says that

Jesus Christ is God. Even after the Father, seen to be no more, yet, people still address Jesus with all the names and nicknames, which they used to treat his Father.

Attention Here:

Idol Worshippers: (traditional religion) these are the oldest sect of faith. They are everywhere in the world today. They actively worship their type of Spirits, which they believe is the leading Creator, who lives in Heaven, hearing and doing wonders for them. Though, with the complaint that since modern religions existed, that is when the whole world started having all kinds of problems here and there. They say that modern people with current beliefs define the land, which is not like that in the days when religions had not come.

Judaism: The Jews believe in the spirits they worship. That made them not to be distracted or to recognize another. So, they only believed in ghosts, who are also in his Throne in Heaven. Judaism, seen to be the foundation of Christianity and, at the same time, one of the smallest faiths in the history of religion.

Christianity: Christians believe their King, the Father (The King of Kings), is seated in his throne in Heaven. His Son, Jesus, is also seated at his right hand. While the earthly Father was Joseph, and the human Mother, Mary, who Christians also believe died and resurrected and are in Heaven, at the right hand interceding on our behalf before the Father. Likewise, Joseph and Mary are negotiating on our behalf too. These are the reasons the Catholics church has a society called Saint Joseph and Saint Mary. We believe that the Father has committed things into the hands of the Son Jesus, according to the book of Philippians 2:9. For these, Christians believe that other faiths, which are not into the kingdom of Jesus, the person or those groups of people, are nowhere, which means that they are still beating around the bush.

Islam: Muslims believe that Allah is also sitting in his throne in Heaven. Now, because of his position, Mohammed, his final messenger, is now in charge of his subjects. They also believe that the Mother of Mohammed –Amine, who lived and passed away, is now in Heaven. They firmly believe that there is no other religion like Islam and there is no other worthy to worship than Allah.

Hinduism: Hindus are also with their own belief that their Shiva(God)), the Father, is also occupying his Throne in Heaven. Including the families, Davis, the wife, Gnash, the first son; and Kumar (Krishna), the immediate brother to Gnash. Also, with Vishnu, an uncle to Gnash, and the Indians, that worship Hindu. Vowed that no human on earth would get any of their members to convince to convert into any sects of religion etc.

If I ask, how many Creators are there in Heaven (Sky)? Or is He only one God? These sect's worship and still critics among each other. While each of these sects' regards different ways of worshipping a lower Creator. So, if it's not a spiritual trick, then my dear, among all these sects of faith stated above, can you help us point out the most rightful one with this spirit? Because we can see that they all have their King of Kings in the Sky (Heaven), and spirit beings are all their Creator. These reasons contributed such long these spirits in operation, deceiving the Entire World without the knowledge of anybody. It seems to have blinded all the faiths not to witness what another set of beliefs are doing. If not, the spirits tricks must have been captured long ago. However, I hope you have not forgotten that we are still on the human language of tales, The Secret of the spirits deceiving the Entire World?

Nevertheless, I feel sorry for all of us who are making spiritual notes or preaching about who the Creator (spirit) is after having discovered their intentions to mankind.

It is likened to someone who lives in the United States of American and has the intention to travel to one of the countries in West Africa. With flight and on the day of the journey, he went to Californian City and boarded a luxurious Bus heading to Japan, with the same intention that he was still on his way to the Country in West Africa. That signifies that for the next one million years to come, the person will always be in the wrong direction. **One of the parables in the scripture, says your ways are not my ways, and your thoughts are not my thoughts, as heaven is above the earth, so my ways above your ways and my thoughts above your thought. So dear, give it a reason?**

Firstly, in his journey, Buses do not travel from the US to Japan. It looks to anybody who is preaching, teaching, or making Spiritual notes as it's written in the scriptures. A Verse of Scripture says many shall be deceived.

(Hosea4:6.) Says that my people will die for lack of knowledge. We finished due to the lack of real understanding of the intention of the Spirits that inspired the Bible writers. That's why a good percentage of the faiths seem to be broke, go to African, Indian, and other Third World Countries, etc., and witness what is going on there through religions because the faiths are banking all hopes on the written words with confidence authorities will do as has written. While it is all parables, the Ancestors use them for illustrations, corrections, instructions, advise, and rebukes, and that's what the Scriptures is all about.

For instance, the Ancestor's proverbs say that a King travels out to a neighbouring Town and comes back with all kinds of presents in his bag. Yes, it happens because he is a giver, and all the people he has given have also given back unto him because he is a giver. That's the real meaning of the Scripture Verse in (Luke6:38). That says, gives and shall be given back unto you, etc. So, that is the reason: Congregations have been putting tithes and offerings in the Churches, hoping to receive back as it's written, without discovering the real intention of the Authorities to those proverbs.

That's why most promises are not coming as expected. It's not a matter of not having enough faith. The Beings that inspired the Bible are unusual spirits and brutal enemies of progress. These are what the Scripture above is all about; check it out. That was the problem of the faiths (the Entire World), no matter what sect of religion you belong to, including the Idol worshippers, which were the foundation and the pillar of the Spirit's business.

Further examples consist of the fact that a lot of the faiths today have the understanding that the congregation of the old beliefs represents today's faiths (Religions). At the same time, also the Heavenly promise that was made to the present trusts represents the promised land of the Old hopes. Again, all the names of the Kings written in the scriptures like King Abraham, King Saul, King David, and King Solomon, etc. represent today's Ministers of the gospels. However, without also having realized that most other things in the scriptures are also in parables (example, illustrations) of what today's Faiths, religions are going to look like in time to come. Mind you, not because the beings inspired by the bible had known the future before they could do that, but in fact, these beings have been following and monitoring the Ancients' way of life and leadership, coupled with the Idol ways of worship for thousands of years, and have ideas of all the procedures, whereby the methods of modern forms of masses are not much different. At the same time, the modern religions have also been in existence without the use of the bible; then later, the guide came into being. Now, with these ideas, these beings can be capable of figuring out what the religions will look like in time to come.

> *If wealth was not involved, Ministers should have years back, discovered all the tricks of the beings against the living:*

RICHEST CHURCHES IN THE WORLD

1. Church of Jesus Christ of Latter-Day Saints- $67. Billon

2. Catholic Church - $30 billion +

3. Catholic Church Australia- $20.9 billion

4. Catholic Church Germany- $25.0 billion

5. Church of England $7.8 billion

6. Opus Dei (part of the Catholic Church) Italy- $2.8 billon

7. Church of Scientology- $2.0 billon

NOW OBSERVE THAT THERE IS NO.....

- » RCCG
- » Winners
- » Christ Embassy
- » Synagogue
- » No Pentecostal church at all

RICHEST PASTORS IN THE WORLD:

1. Bishop Oyedepo - $150 Million

2. Bishop TD Jakes - $147 Million

3. Pastor Chris Oyakhilome - $50 Million

4. Pastor Benny Hinn - $42 Million

5. Pastor Adeboye - $39 Million

6. Pastor Creflo Dollar - $27 Million (He used to be #1)

7. Pastor Kenneth Copeland - $25 Million

8. Evangelist Billy Graham - $25 Million

9. Prophet TB Joshua - $10 Million

10. Pastor Joseph Prince - $5 Million

Observe again that none of the 4 richest churches mentioned have their leaders on this list of the Richest Pastors.

» The Pope is not there.
» The Arch-Bishop of Canterbury is not there.
» The Bishop of Opus Dei is not there.
» The Director of the Church of Jesus Christ of Latter-Day Saints is not there.

NOW OBSERVE AGAIN.

» 6 out of the 10 Richest Pastors are blacks with their congregation being predominantly black
» 4 out of the 10 richest Pastors have their churches in Nigeria, the poverty capital of the world, the 147th most corrupt nation of the world, the home to the

second deadliest terrorist group, the most unsafe place to give birth to in the world

Observe as well that the Richest Churches are situated in

» USA　　　　　» Vatican City　» England

These are amongst the safest, least corrupt and most prosperous Nations.

What a Paradox!! Jesus Christ fed the multitude, but in Nigeria the multitude feed the Men of God and General Overseers.

<u>BBC Africa</u>

<u>Source of Data used: Wikipedia</u>

I will expose the Bible's ways of giving the story to confirm to us that scriptures are full of beings' ideas of tales, which profited nothing from humanity. Please do not forget the written words are inspired by the spirits, which will also help us to witness that the beings involved do not initiate much. Instead, they were coping and imitating humans in whatever we were doing. That's what the Scripture in the book of (Numbers14:28) is all about.

That will also help us to understand that human beings are sensible more than the bible Creator. Again, mind you, this paragraph of the bible's ways of giving tale talks is likely to look more real than those of the humans because the beings inspired, the writers are more con and professional in providing the story. Through their deceitful ways, the writers also had in mind as we do, that is a perfect Creator speaking to them. Without the understanding that the beings involved were all the natural ancestral (familiar) beings that exist among humans. In order to witness this to us,

Here are some examples.

"Nebuchadnezzar the King" made an image of gold, whose height was sixty cubits and its width six cubits. He set it up in the plain of Durra in the province of Babylon and King.

Nebuchadnezzar sent word to gather together satraps, Administrators, Governors, Counsellors, Treasurers, Judges, Magistrates, and all the officials of the provinces. To come to the dedication of the image which King Nebuchadnezzar had set up?

"So satraps, Administrators, Governors, Counsellors, Treasurers, Judges, Magistrates, and all the officials of the provinces gathered together for the dedication of the image King Nebuchadnezzar had set up." Then a herald cried aloud to you, it is commanded, (which means) "Oh people, nations, languages, that at the time you hear the sound of the horn, flute, harp, lyre, and psaltery, in symphony with all kinds of music, you shall fall and worship the gold image that King Nebuchadnezzar has set up."

Whoever does not fall and worship shall be cast immediately into the midst of a burning fiery furnace."

So at that time, when all the people heard the sound of the horn, flute, harp, and lyre in symphony with all kinds of music, all the people, nations, and languages fell and worshipped the gold image which King Nebuchadnezzar had set up." Therefore, at that time, certain Chaldeans came forward and accused the Jews." They spoke and said to King Nebuchadnezzar, "Oh King, live forever. You, oh King, have made a decree that everyone who hears the sound of the horn, flute, harps, lyre, and psaltery in symphony with all kinds of music shall fall and worship the gold image. And whoever does not fall and worship shall be cast into the midst of the burning fiery furnace."

There are certain Jews whom you have set over the affairs of the province of Babylon, Shadrach, Meshach, and Abed-Nego, these men "Oh King have not paid due regards to you, they do not serve your gods or worship the gold image which you have set up. "Then Nebuchadnezzar, in rage and fury, gave the command to bring Shadrach, Meshach, and Abednego, so they brought these Men before the king. "King Nebuchadnezzar Spoke and said to them, 'Is it true, Shadrach, Meshach, and Abednego, that you do not serve my gods or worship the gold image, which I have set up? Now, if you are ready at the time, you hear the sound of the horn. Flute, harps, lyre, and psaltery, in symphony with all kinds of music, you shall fall and worship the image, which I have made. However, if you do not worship, you shall be cast immediately into the midst of a burning fiery furnace. And who is the God who will deliver you from my hand?"

Shadrach, Meshach, and Abednego answered and said to the King, "Oh King Nebuchadnezzar, we do not need to answer you in this matter," If that is the case, our God, whom we serve, can deliver us from the burning fiery furnace. And, he will deliver us from your hand, Oh King." But if not, let it be known to you, oh' King that we do not serve your gods, nor will we worship the gold image which you have set up." Then Nebuchadnezzar was full of fury, and the expression on his face changed towards Shadrach, Meshach, and Abednego. He spoke and commanded that they heat the furnace seven times more than it was usually heated. Also, he commanded certain mighty Men of valour who were in his army to bind Shadrach, Meshach, and Abednego and cast them into the burning fiery furnace.

Therefore, these men were bound in their coats, their trousers, their turbans, and their other garments. Then they were cast into the midst of the burning fiery furnace." Therefore, because the King's command was urgent and the furnace exceedingly hot, the flame killed those men who took up Shadrach, Meshach, and Abednego. And these three men, Shadrach, Meshach, and Abednego, fell bound into the midst of the burning fiery furnace." Then King Nebuchadnezzar was astonished, and he rose in haste and spoke to his counsellors. Did we not cast three men bound into the midst of the fire? They answered and said to the King, "True, oh' King. Look, he answered, I saw four Men lose, walking amid the fire, and they are not hurt, and the form of the fourth is like the son of God."

Then Nebuchadnezzar went near the mouth of the burning fiery furnace and spoke, saying Shadrach, Meshach, and Abednego, servants of the highest, and come out and come here. Then Shadrach, Meshach, and Abednego came out from the midst of the fire." And, the Satraps, Administrators, Governors, and the King's Counsellors gathered together.

They saw these Men, on whose bodies the fire had no power. The hair of their head did not sing, nor were their garments affected. And the smell of fire was not on them. Nebuchadnezzar spoke, saying, "Blessed be the God of Shadrach, Meshach, and Abednego. Who sent his Angels and delivered his servants who trusted in him? And they have frustrated the King's word and yield their bodies. That they should not serve nor worship any other god except their own God..."

Therefore, I make a decree that any people, nations, or languages which speak anything amiss against the God of Shadrach, Meshach, and Abednego shall be cut in pieces, and their houses shall be made an ash heap because there is no other who can deliver like this." Then the King promoted Shadrach, Meshach, and Abednego in the province of Babylon.

That's an example of the bible's language of tales. Okay, now, I would like to point out to us some crucial words for a better understanding of the stories which will witness to us that it's all stories.

Who was King Nebuchadnezzar of Babylon in the bible?

Well, let me put the response this way. King Nebuchadnezzar is like King Joke in the human languages of stories in the land of Israel. He is also like God, the King of Kings in the area of Israel as recorded in the bible, but remembers this does not mean he is special God

Why did "King Nebuchadnezzar" pronounce to gather Governors, Counsellors, Treasurers, Judges, Magistrates, and other officials in provinces of Babylon for the dedication of the image?

I will say the King did that in a way to show His supremacy over his Subjects. That similar to the scripture that says, "At the name of Jesus, all knees must bow in Sky (Heaven), Earth, and under the Earth, which is also, because of his supremacy over his subjects (the Entire World). Because we all believe there is a Creator. So, for the fact, we believed that there is a king of kings. Who is ruling over us, is enough for the King to act otherwise before his subjects?

What does it mean or represent for the King to announce that all the people who refuse to come or hear the sound of the horn and refuse to bow down and worship the King's image shall be cast into the fiery burning furnace?

That also means unbelievers, none religious (the enemies of the King) that have not accepted Jesus Christ in their heart and made a confession that Jesus is Lord and their saviour, refused to worship him as King; that means the sinners, the enemies of Creator, should be cast into the lake of Hellfire on the last day as recorded, because of their disobedient to the King.

What does it represent regarding the individual Jews, Shadrach, Meshach, and Abednego, who were brought before the King Nebuchadnezzar who failed to worship or bow down to the King's image? These names, Shadrach, Meshach, and Abednego, mean the sinners before the King. On judgment day, according to the scriptures, those who disobeyed commandments of the King they belonged to the Hell-fire.

Can you give an example of the meaning of the decree that was set up before the individual Jews, Shadrach, Meshach, and Abednego in the land of Babylon?

That equally means, like in today's religions, as the scriptures say, anyone who did not believe and accepted Jesus as his saviour, is not of him. That means the person or those groups of people do not belong to the Heavenly promise. That means they are enemies because they have rejected the commandments of the King. So, they are like Satan and the Devils, according to what the scriptures said.

GREATEST KING

Who was the son of the Creator, who seems to have saved certain Jews from the burning fiery furnace? As is written, the son means Jesus (Angels), who appears to have saved them.

Nevertheless, mind you, that's a way to show his supremacy over all human kings. Also means that the individual Jews are like the righteous Christians before the King of Israel. Those who have accomplished the commandments of the ruler. That Hellfire is not for them because of their faith, which signifies that the master will surely save them from Hellfire on the last day as promised.

Why did all the officials of the King gather to see what would happen to individual Jews?

They did that to witness the consequences of disobedience, as the scriptures describe how the righteous will stand to see what will happen to the unrighteous in the Hellfire. Cast your mind back to the question in the bible.

Which King Lazarus, the beggar, asked Father Abraham? He wondered, Oh, Father Abraham, will it be possible for me to have a view over the rich Man in the Hellfire. Abraham responded, "No. My son, there is a gap."

Why did the King bless and praise the King of certain Jews for having delivered His servants by his angels?

Yes, the King did that in a way to show subjects that power belongs to the King of the individual Jews. At the same time, mind you that story of the King Nebuchadnezzar, in the bible, was written to show the bible readers what the bible Creator can do in a situation of those who believe in Him. So, let it not leave your mind, for it all spirits stories for more attention to His subjects.

Why did the King promote individual Jews?

It merely represents or refers to what the scripture said about the promotion (Ushering) of the righteous people into Heaven a way to show His supremacy and fulfilment over his Subjects.

Nevertheless, if you look at the meaning of these paragraphs of tale talks. You will be able to understand it's a way of getting people's attention. That's what is happening in the life of the present-day King's, Presidents, Governors, and Queens, etc. That means, in any authority, the person involved will try to show up how powerful he/she is. If Spirit tricks had not been discovered, I should have asked; all these names of Kings in the Bibles, where are their exact today Family roots /offspring? Are there among the Sodom and Gomorrah the bible Creator has destroyed? Do you know in the language of tale talks, if you do not make use of your senses, you will carry aware of believing all things because it will sound real in your ears?

How many today's Ministers have the Creator also blessed mightily to that extent? Now, people of the world are in millions, and today's ways of making wealth are simpler than in those days. Inhabitants are very few. None of these entire bible Kings that have much wealth as recoded was a farmer. Because, mainly in farm work, the Ancestors made their wealth mostly in those days.

FURTHER WAYS OF STORIES;

It is good to caution our ways of thought, especially when we are up-right because some people you look down on, may sometimes become up-right too:

I will also expose these before us. Another bible language of tales to witness that all the bible words are full of stories of the strange beings, which profited nothing to humanity. In other to do that, I will only point out some scriptures.

Here are more examples:

Now, King David was old, advanced in years and they put covers on him, but could not get warm. Therefore, his servants said to him, "Let a young woman, a virgin, be sought for our Lord the King, and let her care for him, and let her lie in your bosom, that our lord the King may be warm." Then King David answered and said, "Call Bathsheba to me." So she came into the King's presence and stood before the King." King took an oath and said, as the Lord lives, which has redeemed my life from every distress." Just as I swore to you by the Lord of Israel, saying, "Assuredly, Solomon, your son shall be king after me, and he shall sit on my throne in my place, so I certainly will do this for you this day."

Then Bathsheba bowed with her face to the earth, and paid homage to the king, and said, "Let my lord King David live forever." Then Zadok, the Priest, took a horn of oil from the Tabernacle and anointed Solomon as a king. Then they blew the horn, and all the people said, "Long live King Solomon. Now Oh' Lord, my God, you have made your servant king instead of my Father David, but I am a little child; I do not know how to go out or come in. And your servant is in the midst of your people whom you have chosen. Great people, too numerous to be numbered or counted. Therefore, give your servant an understanding heart to judge your people so that I may discern between good and evil. For, who can judge these great people of yours?"

The speech pleased the Lord that Solomon had asked this thing. Then he said to him, "Because you have asked this thing, and have not asked long life for yourself, nor have you asked riches for yourself, nor have you asked the life of your enemies, but have asked for yourself understanding to discern justice"?

Greatest Mistake

Behold, I have done according to your words. See, I have given you a wise and understanding heart so that there has not been anyone like you. Before you, nor shall any like you arise after you. "I also have given you what you have not asked, both riches and honour, so that there shall not be anyone like you among the kings all your days.

Now, two women who were harlots came to the King and stood before him, saying, "One woman said, o' my Lord, this woman and I dwell in the same house, and I gave birth while she was in the house. Then it happened: the third day after I gave birth, this woman also gave birth. And we were together; no one was with us in the house except two of us."

This woman's son died at night because she lay on him. So, she arose in the middle of the night and took my son from my side while your maidservant slept. Put him in her bosom and laid her dead child in my bosom. When I rose in the morning to nurse my son, there he was, dead. However, when I had explained to him in the morning, indeed, he was not my son whom I had born. Then the other woman said, "No. But the living one is my son, and the dead one is your son," And the first woman said. No. But the dead one is your son and the living one is my

Greatest King

son." Thus, they spoke before the King. The king said, "The one that says, this is my son, who lives, and your son is the dead one, and the other says. Not. But your son is the dead one. And my son is the living one. Then the King said. Bring me a sword." So they brought a sword before the King.

Furthermore, the king said, "Divide the living child in two, and give half to one and give half to the other." Then the woman whose son was living spoke to the king, for she yearned with compassion for her son; and she said "Oh my lord, give her the living child, and by no means kill," but the other said, "Let him be neither mine nor yours, but divide him." So the king answered and said, "Give the first woman the living child, and by no means kill him, she is his mother." All Israel heard of the judgment, which the king had rendered, and they feared the king, for they saw that the wisdom of the creator was in him to administer justice.

King Solomon had twelve Governors all over Israel, who provided food for the King and his household. Each one made provision for one month of the year.

Greatest Mistake

> **"** *The weight of gold that came to Solomon yearly was six hundred and sixty-six talents of gold.* **"**

Besides that, comes from the travelling merchants from the income of traders. From all the kings of Arabia and Governors of the Country, the King made a great Throne of Ivory and overlaid it with pure Gold. The Throne had six steps; the top of the Throne was round at the back. There was Armrest on either side of the palace of the seat, and two Lions stood beside the armrests. Twelve lions stood there, one on each side of the six steps. Nothing like this has made for any other kingdom.

All kings Solomon's drinking vessels were pure Gold. "Not one was Silver; that's accounted as nothing in the days of

King Solomon." For the King had merchant's ships at Sea with the fleet of Hiram, once every three years, the merchant ships came bringing Gold Silver, Ivory apes and Monkeys." So King Solomon surpassed all the Kings of the Earth in riches and Wisdom."

Nevertheless, King Solomon loved many foreign women, as well as the daughters of Pharaoh, women of Moabites, Ammonites, Edomites, Sidonians, and Hittites. "From the nation of whom the Lord had said to the children of Israel, you shall not intermarry with them, or they with you. Surely, they will turn away your hearts after their gods, and Solomon clung to these in love. "And he had seven hundred wives, princesses, and three hundred concubines, and his wives turned away his heart." For it was so when Solomon was old, that his wives turned his heart after other gods, and his heart was not loyal to the Lord, his God, as it was in the heart of his father, David. "Solomon did evil in the sight of the Lord and did not fully follow the Lord as his father David did."

For a full understanding, which will also help us to realize that it's all stories from the unusual beings before the Entire World and not only before the faiths?

In Details:

"Who was King David in the land of Israel?

As I said earlier, the names of kings in Israel, written in the scriptures, are all the same. That does not apply to a particular person. These are why family roots cannot be found because it is copied by the unusual spirits (the deceivers of man) from the ancient's ways of leaderships, for deception and, in a way, to make it look like it is these spirits of God, who initially created it be. So, the name "King David in the Land of Israel Is like God the King of Israel." "Jesus, the King of Kings and the Lord of Lords in the land of Israel," King Joke in the land of Israel, King Nebuchadnezzar of Babylon (of Israel or the entire World)" etc. However, due to the deception of the beings, it sounds real before our ears because the unusual spirits that are acting as Creator are right here on earth with us; they can whisper/speak to you as a person or through the Minister of the gospels.

Names of kings in the bible are a kind of an illustration of today's Minister of the gospels, and not that there is a particular King David in the scripture existed before, no."

What did you understand for a young virgin woman to be with King David as a helping hand?"

The virgin woman brought to King David was not supposed to be strange to many of us because I have already said that the spirits do not initiate anything of their own making, rather they imitate human ways of life. So that's our way of life. There will be a time in life after parents bring up their children. When parents age, the children will not continue staying with them. They are likely to leave their parents, let alone the King, for their own making (start their own families), and since they have the right, you cannot expect the parents to be alone without a helping hand in their old age. I remember when I lived with my grandparents. At that time, both of them had clocked 76 years of age. I was giving them every necessary help as I could in those days. Thus, likewise was the virgin woman that brought to be with King David.

Why did King David request Bathsheba to come to him for specific instructions?

Well, I will say King David did that for the love he had for Bathsheba and her son Solomon. Also, witnesses to us that David had advanced in age, which happens these days, too. When some parents get very old, they would like to create fortune/wealth for their children to avoid misunderstanding after their father seems no more.

Had he not done that, Solomon would likely not have been the next King after David in the land of Israel because King David also had other sons from other women.

What did you understand by Bathsheba to bow her face to the earth and proclaimed her best wishes to David the King?

Yes, she did that before the King for honouring the King for the fulfilment of his promise. That allowed King Solomon to take over the throne after King David. Even though King Solomon may not be the next in the throne in the house of David, but since the King so loved Bathsheba and had earlier vowed to Bathsheba that her son would be on his throne after him. Again, the godly character of Bathsheba, by bowing her head down before the King supposed taught us, what she did also signifies the ways people (the ancestors) in those days used to worship their traditional kings. That was where the Spirits imitated and by tricks introduced it before the ancestors, mode to worship the creator who is in heaven.

Likewise, the faiths are doing today before the church altar. Though, it now looks as if is spirits who first made it be, while it was the traditional ways of humans worshipping kings in ancient time and now in many places.

What do you think were the reasons for King Solomon to marry 700 wives and have 300 concubines?

Anyway, I can say that's the character of the people in authorities, mostly the Ancient Time's Kings. The ancient kings were known to have many wives and concubines, but not to this extent of high numbers that made up for more attention of which all of us should reason.

How do you reason the twelve governors in the land of Israel, who provide food for the king every month?

Personally, even when their tricks had not discovered, I doubted that verse of the scriptures. Reasons are these; the twelve governors were the governors that were also under the leadership of the president, King Solomon, in the land of Israel. It is like, in a country, after, the president, they still have 12 governors or more depending, for the states, which are under the leadership of the president. Which is likely for the governors to be visiting the president; likewise, the faiths are doing today before the church altar. Though, it now looks as if is spirits who first made it be, while it was the traditional ways of humans worshipping kings in ancient time and now in many places.

Yes, for the governors to be visiting the president frequently, even to his house, as the president seems to be overall king, of which you know the governors will never visit the president (whole king) empty-handed and. No one will expect governors going in pairs when visiting the president. Whatever you see in the bible was copied from humans' ways/ideas of living their life.

What did you understand about Lions, King Solomon had in his palace?

"It's all self-praising of the people in power to show his supremacy and self-esteem because he believed that he is the king and had wealth and nothing is too difficult for Him a King. But that is unbelievable because lions are very violent and dangerous to be with human beings, or have you see any king at this present age that has lions in his household? It's difficult, even now, the ways of shepherding dangerous animals are easier due to civilization."

The riches and honour which the Lord added to "King Solomon" what does it signify?

Well, the riches and honour of King Solomon are effortless to understand, so far we have discovered the value of the beings involved, though in those days, never a time.

Kingship meant for the poor even now that is what we should realize despite the fact, that's written to witness us that nothing is impossible with the bible Creator.

Why did King Solomon pray for Wisdom?

King Solomon did that because that is the attitude of every human King which started from the ancients Kings, due to problems and difficulties, the subjects would bring before the King. Also, in human understanding, Solomon did that because we believe that there is a Creator, that nothing will be impossible with Him.

What is the difference between the spirits that do a miracle through the modern religious ministers and the beings that do wonders through the Idol priest (traditional) ministers?

Well, beings all over the entire universe are the same. Their original name is the natural ancestral (familiar) spirits. They first started the religious business with ancestors, and they are also the being's behinds any secret societies. As humans all over the world are the same type of humans and able to future in different ways, so are the spirits beings. Moreover, this is one of the thing that is supposed to witness to all the faiths that it's all tale talks because since I have been an adult, I have never heard the idol worshippers mention going to Heaven after death while they too believe that Creator exists. The same beings started the worship business with them.

Well, I think that the reasons are simple. It seems that the promise of Heaven made after the son of the sign, Jesus came and died, resurrected, and ascended into Heaven as recorded, which the foundation of the New Testament bible is. However, in the Old Covenant (Old Testament), a the promise of land that was filled with milk and honey was made to people in those days — the children of Israel, which they did not enter.

Though, these days, the faiths believed and magnify things written in the bible with hope spirits inspired, due to deception. Some of the disciples now regarded the idol Priest ways of worshipping as lower Spirits (god), which is the belief of Devils.

What made the spirits magnify the tales of the King even up to this modern era?

I have said earlier; the giver of the tales would only succeed by furthering the stories if the receivers believe what the teller is saying. So, the spirits had no choice than magnifying the stories because of the faiths, the congregation, and the entire world. believes what the scriptures say, that if you can only accept, then it will happen to you. The Scripture says that Abraham believed him, and then it was accounted for you, righteousness. Likewise, because the people involved except the conviction words of the nonentity, that there is a Creator. Then the beings had no choice than to continue magnifying the stories of the King. Even to the point of providing ways for the third and fourth Testament Bibles, in the book of Revelation, that taught about the New Jerusalem, where death will be no more.

Why are commandments and decrees in all the illustrations of the tale above?

I think it's quite simple in town, country, and even in some big organizations. There is likely to be a leader who represents the king. Because, the mirror of the Spirit, through the initiatives, utterances of men and women of this age. We all understand that whenever there is a leadership (king), there is also likely to be rules and authorities, commandment, decrees, laws, and so on for better achievements.

How do the Familiar Spirits manage to read our inner mind and understand the thoughts of Men?

They can do that because they are spirits and able to be in any part of our body without our awareness. For example, if you want to whisper an issue/something to somebody, it is likely, the person will have to come closer to you. Also, if possible, you will face your mouth towards the ear of that individual so that people around will not hear what you are whispering. Then, whatever you say, the person will listen to it.

That is the way the spirits hear and understands the inner mind of men. Because whatever one meditates, it would immediately join/echo up with air, then the most wicked one called the devil.

Are very close, monitoring you 24 hours would be able to hear it. It's not that humans have a spirit inside their bodies, which helps them to read our inner mind, and this is the most reason why spirits are at all-time, very close to every individual in the universe without choice. Which helps them give an account of every single person at any moment which qualifies them answering the Bible authorities, even in my observation if it is allowed for some other animals to be getting closer to humans as the Spirits World does? Then they will be capable of reading man to a large extent. Because many Animals understand when we talk to them, for example, the wild birds, dog, pigeons, parrots, chimp's camels, and even the bush carts also remember the story of Hezekiah and his donkey in the bible?

What made human beings believe that beings created us?

I will say that it's because of the characteristics of the familiar spirits towards humans, which are not common to Man's knowledge. Such beings are in existence, operating to the extent of reading the mind of Man without Man's perception. They are also able to remind you or me of the

Past, even when you may have forgotten about it, spirits are also able to speak any language; in short, only for a reason they did not easily seem and can convince a man by operating through the manners of men without our knowledge. Again, reading the mind of men is enough for humans to believe there is a creator; hence, Man has not discovered anything else capable of this.

Why are kings in all the bibles and also in the human's language of tales?

Because the stories of a human king were copied by the beings for deception, right from the people in those days, and also, the story of a king is something a teller will be giving many people would like to listen. You cannot stand before a group of people telling them stories about a poor man or a nonentity; many will not want to hear.

However, when you open up telling something about a king, how a king ruled in a particular time, by giving them every compelling story of the wealth of the king. How everything the king uses in his palace is of pure gold, and all the good things happening in the king's palace, you will be

Surprised that many of the people around will not allow you to depart without concluding.

Another point is that the name King would mostly be the head stories because it's all tale talks; these are also the primary reasons you can see all the Kings written in the religious bibles. For example, can you imagine even Lazarus, the beggar in the Scripture who has not got anything, who used to be at the doorstep of King Abraham in the Scripture, also known and addressed as king Lazarus in Heaven as written in the bible book of (Luke 16:19)? The scriptures say that there was a certain rich man who was clothed in purple and fine linen and fared sumptuously every day. However, there was a certain beggar named Lazarus, full of sores, who was laid at his gate, desiring to feed with the crumbs which fell from the rich Man's table? Moreover, the dogs came and licked his sores.

"So it was that the beggar died and was carried by Angels to Abraham's bosom. The rich Man also died and was buried" Also, being in torment in hell, he lifted his eyes and saw Abraham afar off. Lazarus in his bosom, then he (the rich Man) cried and said: "Father Abraham, have mercy on me, and send Lazarus that he may dip the tip of his finger in water and cool my tongue for being in torment in his flame." Abraham said, "Son, remember, in your lifetime, you received your good things. Likewise, Lazarus received evil things. Nevertheless, now, he is comforted, you tormented," besides, between you and us, there is an excellent guff fixed here. So, those who want to pass from here cannot nor can those from there give to us.

If not tales, look at Lazarus, the beggar in the bible. Just because he believed, staying at the doorstep of King Abraham, and for this, it accounted for his righteousness in Heaven. Moreover, somewhere in scripture says that He has made us kings and priests, and we shall reign in his world. Why? Because we believed in him and for that, He has accepted all the faiths, as kings and priests unto him because the subjects have not seen him physically and yet believed in him. However, even though he has said that still does not make us the real king here on earth because name king is mostly used in the language of tales for more attention. For the fact that the spirits involved are the imitators of humans. That whenever there is a king, that means Governments, commandment, leaderships authorities, requirements, and so many other things will be involved. There will never be a time when there will be all these officials in a town country, and then you expect just an ordinary human being to be their leader. I do not think that makes sense.

Greatest King

Finally, in these paragraphs stated above, we can witness that in all the tale talks, before any decrees, authorities, or commandments that the Kings made, there were already people, subjects (societies), and not just one or two people. So, the Kings above did not create authorities or decrees without having many people before them. Even in today's human governments, before any government can create laws, there will/must be many people, societies, either to obey the rules or to walk against it.

In the human language of the tale above, before King Joke could make a decree, there were already many people (subjects) before him. Again, in the bible's ways of tales, before King Nebuchadnezzar could make his decree, there were also many people (His subjects). Neither to obey nor to walk against it. The same things occur in the tale language of King Solomon.

AFTER MY HEART

It is quite understandable that, in a sense, before any law will abide and guide anything, which will attract authority to come up with specific requirements to guide those things before societies. Yes, what I'm trying to point out is, before the Spirits of the Entire Religion had ordered, instructed or, decrees before the Bible, Adam and Eve, not to tamper with the apple tree amid in the Garden. There were already people(Societies) right here on Earth and not just only Adam and Eve. Why? Because these authorities operate through the ideas of humans. So, there is no way a decree that will govern the societies (the entire world) will be created just before one or two people. Therefore, my main point is that people have been much in existence. That means that Adam and Eve are not the first humans here on earth as recorded in the scriptures, which means these bible authorities are not the Creator of Man. Another excellent point that exposes their plans to humanity in things of religions.

However, we have discovered unnecessary rules in the scripture that are not good to Man.

So, as we have said, whatever we are doing, the beings are also doing it much more, like if somebody can be jealousy over your Progress today, Spirits can also do much more:

Illustrations:

"Now a great war broke out in Heaven, Michael and his Angels fought with the dragon and his Angels: but they did not prevail, nor was a place found for them in heaven any longer. So the dragon was cast out that serpent of old, called the Satan, who deceives the whole world. He cast to the earth, and his angels cast out with him." (Rev, 12.7.)

Attention Here:

Story imitated by the beings, enemies of the ancient time king's ruling of a town, who regarded before his people/subjects as all-powerful because of his righteousness and holiness. That is the fundamental issue in today's religions, as explained. Satan and his angels in the bible, who are the enemies of the King of righteousness and holiness, represent The King's Enemies in Ancient Times.

Further illustrations:

In my town, concerning our present town king, there are about two or three villages that are not in support of his leadership in every aspect. I hope you know what that means? Among those villages, one person is heading them, who represents Satan, and he is likely to be the very one that the traditional King (God) will recognize most. Whatever faults the King will place against those villages (the unbelievers), the name of their leader will come up first or will first be mentioned. Like the name of Satan Is being mentioned everywhere by the faiths. Remember that those villagers who are against the government of the present/active King are with one accord. If it happens, war breaks out between the two parties, the villagers (the faiths) that are in support of the present/active King will prevail because they are the majority in number.

However, if in the case the King concluded subjects (the faiths) that their enemies should depart their town or the

King's palace (heavenly place). That will, immediately, or if the present King decides to put them in prison.

They will capture leaders first, who represents Satan, and will be imprisoned at the worst place (bottom pitch of hell) with chains. Also, if the king later decides to release them for some time and some fresh air. They will continue to discourage others from the corrupt government of the present/active king.

The book of Revelation describes how Satan will be put in chains for One thousand years. Later, he will be released. However, I do not know if you are a witness to this. I mean, the modern way of maltreating prisoners for their disobedience is to put them in prison for a couple of years. Sometimes, the prison officer will bring them out for some fresh air. After that, they will be taken back to their prison quarters. That is the way the scriptures describe the bible King will handle Satan and his agents. He was imitated by these beings and will later release them for more deception on the people of the king (the faiths). So, whatever you see in any religious book today was imitated from ancient ways of life and leadership for deception by the spirits that are familiar to Man.

Greatest Mistake

This photo was taken in 1998, demonstrating the author's good health and wellbeing while being a committed pentecostal church worker.

It made us understand that one of the apostles of Jesus Christ called Judas betrayed him to Pontius Pilate with 30 pieces of silver. (Matthew 27:3), which imitated from the human way of life (Proverbs), which says; that only people who know you (your closest) will plan your downfall, not the outsiders.

Moreover, it says that Jesus was betrayed with 30 pieces of silver by Judas to Pontus- Pilate, likewise, in those days even now, the ancestors (Idol worshippers) used to purchase the goat or the Lamb of Redemption with money (silver).

It's written; that Jesus asked to pay tax by Pharisees, according to the book of Matthew. That is imitated from the system of human governments, like the example of many Cities in African Countries.

Along the road, there will be tax collectors cueing up waiting for the taxpayers. Any mature man who comes across will be held (caught) and will be asked or forced the person to pay his tax. The way, the system in most of the third-world countries to this day.

In the same chapter, (Verse 18), Jesus came across a tree and found no fruit on it but Leaves, and he cursed the tree saying from now on, let no fruit grow on you ever again, and the fig tree withered, and the disciples marvelled. That imitated.

You too should know that during the dry season (winter), trees wither and lose all their leaves, and it's also not all trees that bear fruits. Everyone knows that, and no one should claim to have made it that way, but it's Nature.

The death of Jesus on the cross for our sins is unknown to many. A parable, encouraged by the Spirits, Familiar to Man. Perhaps you know the Ancient (and even till today in third world countries) traditional ways of killing goats and sometimes pouring their blood into a hole dug in the ground (liberation). After sacrifice, they gig whole hang the goat on a thick stick in the shape of a cross with the two hands extended on both sides. They tie or nail it up to roast the underside well. Also, keep in mind that the goat is likely to be purchased with money. Likewise, the Pilate bought (purchased) him (Jesus) for 30 pieces of silver from Judas. This ancient tradition still takes place in third-world countries.

Then, after the accusations against Jesus, He was killed and hung up (nailed) with both arms extended against the cross. As our ancestors did the goat of libation, so too they did Jesus, when families, as instructed by the chief priest or an oracle. Brought goats to the shrines as idols for Sacrifice, they – adults and children alike – would hiss and mock the goat because the goat will kill that day. So to do the scriptures relate how the very same events. Befell on Jesus, people against him spat on him, mocked and hit him after his trial and sentence.

Remember, just as the goat cries out before it killed at the point of death. So, too, Jesus did as he cried out, "La ma shabattan!" Just as the ancient goat of libation sacrificed before the shrine for sins committed. Thus, as the scriptures record, it is the representation of Jesus, nailed on the cross for all our sins through the ages from Adam and Eve onwards. Our ancestors valued the blood of their goats, from which they would make sauces or soups out of it after sacrifice. In the same way, Christians value the blood of Jesus so powerfully, sprinkling it all over the body by faith through prayer.

We can see that through the stick that our ancestors used to mount their goats are the image of a cross, and likewise, the cross of Jesus. While the thorns on the head of Jesus represent a symbol of the yam thorns, our ancestors used when sacrificing the goat to roast its crown very well. All of this occurred, and it was all as a punishment for sins committed. Thus, can we understand that the beings Familiar to Man operate in the same manner, using old ideas and ways?

Jesus' death and stories were not a physical event. The spirits inspired the bible writers through visions and dreams. This is why it merely contains tales and little

Greatest Mistake

value in terms of religion, except for the fact that ministers of the gospel are favoured. For example, as the scriptures describe, only leaders Joshua and Caleb entered the Promised Land from out of the assembles of the children of Israel during their wilderness.

A further example: It says, "To registered with Mary, his betrothed wife, who was with a child. So, it was, while they were there, the days completed for her to deliver. She brought forth her firstborn son in a Manger (Luke2:5-7)." Yes, but does it make any difference, without recalling, in the ancient times, when there were no hospitals, any time women were due to deliver a baby. They did that in the manger, in yam barns, or even in the bush garden, and they were doing that because there was no secure place, not alone in having a hospital as we do today. So, whatever you see in the bible was imitated or copied from the old way of life for deceptions by the beings that are familiar to Man.

Right today, we have discovered all the stories to be otherwise. In the book of (Exodus2:3) says that Moses was born by a woman and, after she could not hide him anymore, took an arc of bulrushes for him, daubed it with asphalt and pitch, put the child in it, and laid it in the reeds by the river's bank.

(Verse 5:) Then the daughter of Pharaoh came down to bathe at the river, and her maidens walked along the riverside, and when she saw the ark among the reeds, she sent her maid to get it.

Verse 6: And when she opened it, she saw the child, and behold, the baby wept, so she had compassion on him and said, this is one of the Hebrews' Children. And she nursed the child.

It was copied from the ancient ways of some young females who accidentally got pregnant. Also, they could not abort after giving birth and not being able to care for the child due to circumstances. Control would dump the baby in rubbish bins or by the banks of a river for water to carry the child; some may even decide to put the baby in a pitch toilet, and conclude to tell a lie that she miscarried so that people around will not take notice.

ULTIMATE SECRET

In the book of (Exodus 33:20), God (spirit) told Moses that he is not able to see His face, for no man shall see me and live. However, spirits are like ordinary air or wind, which cannot be seen easily. Remember also that spirit beings do not have bodies like humans. It is mentioned in the book of (Luke 24:39) "So the spirits that claimed Creator (Ancestral Spirits) have no back or front and have no face, but He said that to Moses because of the face and the back human beings and other living things are having, so that means he was not in truth with Moses." Here is another example of the meaning of that verse, as stated above. In those days, if somebody said to you that he would not allow you to see his/her face but would only allow you to see his back, that's an idiom word; his face simply means that he is not going to be honest with you, while his back means that he will only be telling you one thing or the other so as to deceive you, the spirits are operating according to the characters of humans, which enable them familiar to Man.

Familiar Spirit read and understands our inner mind, so please think twice before action for them sometimes contribute to your thinking

It says, "Let women keep silent in the church for they are not permitted to Speak." (1corinthians 14:34). Well, you too will be a witness that any existing minister of the gospels these days that are the founders of any church, most likely the wife has become a minister as well. There is an adage which says that where there is a successful man, there will be a successful woman around him. Or do you want to tell me that it is not the same spirits that inspired the bible that is still in operation in those churches? Well, as we all know, that truth is constant, but I am here to tell you that is written due to the jealousy of the beings. That made them say that women would not stand before the Congregation so that men in the Congregation would not take notice because the spirit has been too cunning and not powerful enough to stop them due to today's civilization, then, they ignored because there is nothing they can do anymore, and today's women are doing whatever they like in the churches, even to the point of single women setting and planting churches.

Now it came to pass when men began to multiply on the face of the earth, and daughters were born to them. That the sons of God (familiar spirits) saw the daughters of men's jealousness that they were beautiful, and they took wives for themselves of all whom they chose. The Lord said my spirits should not strive with Man forever, for he is indeed flesh, yet his days shall be one hundred and twenty years (jealousy of these authorities against men and women of this age).

There were giants on the earth in those days, and also afterward when the sons of the King (familiar spirits) came into the daughters of men (spiritual husbands), and they bore children to them. Those were the mighty men who were of old men's renown. Then the Lord saw that the wickedness of Man was great on the earth and that every thought of his heart was only evil continually. Also, the Lord was sorry that he had made Man on the planet. He grieved in his heart. So the Lord said, "I would destroy man whom I have created from the face of the Earth, Man, and Beasts, creeping things and the Birds of the air, for I am sorry, that I have made them." However, Noah found grace in the eyes of Him.

In those days,

Please, when you get to this very chapter, ensure you have your bible with you to witness "I did not make it up." That's what we preach daily before assembly. Well, in the life of professional liars, there are too many things you could find there. Let me ask the women this question. Is there anything that your child, whom you carried for nine months, will do to you, and you decide to end up his/her life? Okay, remember the frightening story of two women who brought with a child case before King Solomon? Anywhere the story is preached before the faiths, people will be amazed.

I do not know what you understand by the word "when the sons of the king came into the daughters of men." Be aware that the sons mentioned mean the Familiar Spirits. It also shows us how jealous these authorities are, especially of our women. So, men, be advised of your spouse/partner. Whatever is good for you, likewise to these authorities?

Lastly, in the boasting of the professional liars, it says, "Now I saw a new Heaven and a new earth, for the first heaven and the first earth had passed away, and the sea was no more. Then I, John, saw the Holy City, New

Jerusalem, coming down out of Heaven from Him, prepared as a bride, adored for her husband. And I heard a loud voice from heaven saying, behold the tabernacle of Him is with men, and he will dwell with them, and they shall be his people. He will be with them and be their King, and He will wipe away every tear from their eyes; there shall be no more death, nor shall there be sorrow, nor crying, there shall be no more pain, for the former things have passed away."

Boasting of the beings in revelation in time to come, boasting of the professional liars: Okay, we have discovered a lot of things that will quickly help us to conclude this very passage without wasting much of our time and put it where it belongs. One point is, we have discovered that what scripture is talking about is the space/sky, which the scientists have been in and out, and found another planet where life does not exist, which the bible did not talk. Again, we have also found out that the spirit did not engage the Virgin Mary to have Jesus. Likewise, Elizabeth did not bring John the baptize into this world. Then, how can we will believe in the gospels of John? These are the simple questions we need to answer ourselves.

Attention here:

In real understanding, most of the things that they use for deceiving us are most of the present things that have already been in existence here on Earth. Further, is a scripture somewhere in the bible that talks about the death of Moses, in the bible book of (Jude1:9). "Yet, Michael the Archangel in contending with the devils, when he disputed about the body of Moses, dared not bring against him a reviling accusation but said the Lord rebuke you. Because the devil came in to have his body and angels of the King also came and rebuked the devils."

In understanding, it is likening to the present-day Christians. Suppose a minister, previous in his lifetime, had disobeyed, and all the people/brethren are aware of this. Then, after his death, the non-believers (the pagans) will come to claim his body to bury him because he had been cast out by the Christians. After all, he backslides. While the Christians, the Angels, insist that the Minister's body belongs to them

Because he is still a Christian, even though he may have disobeyed, but he is still a Christian. That's a distinctive example of what is happening in third- world countries. In the village, when a backslid Christian dies, the Pagans will gather in a way the body belongs to them. While the Christians will also gather, claiming the person was a Christian when he was alive, as have been said. Most of the things they use to deceive us are mostly the things happening in our present time and what has been in existence here on earth. Memorize on this (Numbers14: 28). Once more, there was a time back home in Africa. Some of the relatives that have passed on for so long, it happens that sometimes "A villager will be given relatives information that somebody comes out Ghost in the area where she/he lived. The dead person frequently appeared as a ghost/spirit, and immediately, somebody takes notice. The Ghost will disappear from view. That is caused by ancestral (familiar) spirits, which are not different from the spirits behind all religions, which was also born and brought up just like everyone in that village as said earlier.

They have been operating in that village and also know everything that is going on there. Also, those beings were doing this because those villagers believed that at times somebody who died would still come out as a ghost. Mostly, those wicked people when they died.

So, because of their belief, the beings monitoring those 24hrs took the records. So the familiar spirits born and brought in that village use ghosts, putting them in fear until something tangible is done. But without the understanding that those beings are not different from others and have no single power to harm them. That's one of the reasons.

Sometimes, when such a thing happens, the people concerned will decide to invite religious Ministers. In order not to spend money, even though, still, after prayer and other things. The dead spirits as recognized, will always be on view until something very, very serious that will cost them a lot of money is done. Without that, it does not make sense to the spirits, the authorities of the Entire Religion. Why? Because most villagers have been deceived by accepting the souls that have been coming out, as the Spirits of their relatives that passed on long ago.

So, for this, it must cost them something serious before they stop coming out on view. Huge families, mostly in third-world countries, have borrowed and wasted a lot of money to get such things sorted out. Without the fact even if they do not, compromise does not prevent their family or village achievements. All these are the wickedness of the beings, the human's opposition.

Therefore, in a sense, I'm here to announce that Adam and Eve means a young man and a young woman who fall in love in ancient times. Ancestors see that as an abomination because of tradition and because the beings are masters of imitation, capitalized on for deceit of humans' sin against the bible king. So, Adam and Eve, as recorded, were not the first people on earth. However, that was written due to the jealousy of the beings against men and women of this era.

Take note, men and women. That what is right for you is also good for the beings that are familiar to us, spiritual husband. Remember what I said about spiritual husbands and how they operate? Anything we are doing, they are copying and doing it likewise. These are the reasons they are familiar to humans. That's a witness; bible scriptures are full of idioms, tales, and proverbs. The ancestors use for advice, corrections, instructions, rebuking, and these are what scriptures are.

(1Corrianthians1:26) "For you see your calling, brethren, that not many wise according to the flesh, not many mighty, not many noble, are called. (V: 27) but has chosen the foolish things of the World to put to shame the wise, and he has chosen the weak things of the World to put shame the mighty things. (V: 28) And the basic things of the World and things that are despised (spirits) He has chosen and the things, which are nothing to bring to nothing the things, that are mighty (humans)"

Well, I do not know if you are getting some revelations from these proverbs. This passage, scripture, mostly believers, due preaches/talks with the hope; the scripture is talking against the unbelievers, especially the well-off men of the World. That regarded the faiths (believers) that are serving the Creator. At the same time, they are weak/poor, and He has also used those foolish things (the believers) as seen by the riches, which are mighty before the king, to make fools of them riches even to the points of not knowing Creator (the king) neither his words.

Still, the real meaning of these sayings as understood is this—the ancestral (familiar) spirit, which inspired the bible, is making mockeries of human beings. You and I, because ancestral spirits have been deceiving us for many years, are the most foolish and hopeless things you can think of that have ever existed. This supposed counted nothing before humans (might) and their knowledge. So, that's why it says, "He (spirits) has used/chosen the foolish things (spirits) of this world to put to shame the wise (humans) because human beings are wiser than the spirits (the authorities of religions) and are also smarter than every other living thing that exists. He has repeated that He uses/chosen the weakest (spirits) something of this world to put to shame the things that are mighty (humans). The lowest of the world it represents The Spirits (The authorities of religions) because the spirits are deceiving us, through religion, that there is a creator who lives in the sky (heaven). Are supposed to be counted as nothing before Humans, and still they were making fools of us - the mighty by deceiving us; this is because Humans are wiser than the Spirits and are also smarter than every other living thing.".

The Following Paragraphs Are Stated by The Late Rev. "Billy' G'

This was the very question the great Apostle Paul answered as he stood before the people of the city of Athens. He had walked its streets and observed their customs. This pagan society had a niche for every God in the world. Yet, their moral corruption was revealed by the hundreds of idols illuminated by the sun at a place called Mars Hill in ancient Greece. Paul spoke with power before this congregation and acknowledged all of their gods and even the unknown God, who is none other than God's Son, the Lord Jesus Christ, who had died for their sins and risen to new life.

Paul declared, "Men of Athens, I perceive that in all things you are very religious; for as I was considering the objects of your worship, I even found an altar with this inscription: to the unknown God. Therefore, the One whom you worship without knowing, Him I proclaim to you" (*Acts* 17:22-23).

What a marvellous declaration. The people of Athens had not stopped to consider their dark side. They had been too busy making gods like themselves.

Our society worships gods of our own making. Our culture is saturated with the worship of sports, sex

, and pleasure. We are busy humanising God and deifying Man. Our idols are not statues of gold and marble; our idols come from the things we love the most. Life does not have to be filled with such emptiness, but we can fill our minds and hearts with the things that bring glory to the Lord Jesus Christ. One who truly follows Him will have a hunger to worship Him, which brings hope and gives salvation.

Above is human understanding, but this is the bottom line of the three paragraphs above, these are words of proverbs to churches from Apostles Paul (today's Ministers) stood amid the Areopagus (Congregation) nd said, "Men of Athens, I perceive in all things, you are very religious. (*Verse* 23) For as I was passing through considering the objects of your worships. I even found an altar with this inscription; "To unknown Creator, therefore, the one whom."

Here are two more examples of characters of the spirits from years ago during one of the Churches where I worshipped. It happened one Sunday morning during the worker's meeting; one of our Pastors shared with the workers that most of the time, whilst the family is preparing to go to the Church for service. One of the children, a daughter about four to five years old; sometimes the daughter will ask the Mom why all the time going to the Church, going to the Church that there is no God; the little girl will ask the Mom to show her a witness that there is God? The Mom will laugh it off and tell her you are still a kid and that the time will come when she will understand; sometimes, the Mom will ask her who Created you? Sometimes, the little girl replied how did you know God Created her? That there is no evidence of it.

The paragraph above is analogous to what Apostle Paul told the Men of Athens. I perceive that you are very religious, for as I considered the objects of your worship, I even found an altar with this inscription to the unknown God.

Mates, the character of the spirits is wonderful. Nothing moves them, so far as human beings are concerned. Though the main point is that tricks have not been known to anybody, these are reasons they have been giving us signs in different ways that there is no Creator. The spirits that monitor Paul use him to address the congregation in the same way the spirits that monitor the little girl use her to tell the Mom that there is no Creator. These are the characteristics of familiar spirits worldwide.

I perceive that in all things, you are very religious, for as I was considering the objects of your worship, I even found an altar with this inscription: to the unknown God.

Another example is this, I could remember one time ago, one of the big American ministers of the Gospels, a senior Minister, was invited to preach in our Church. So, whilst sharing the gospel message of the Holy Spirits before the congregation. He said last week weekend, on Saturday nights, whilst sitting in the sitting room, the daughter was inside her room, preparing to go to a nightclub. Later, the daughter came to him and said," Dad, please come and accompany her to the nightclub? He replied to her have you forgotten I am a Minister of God? But do you know the Man of God later the Holy Spirits spoke to him to accompany the daughter to the night Club, that it doesn't matter? -and doesn't deny him what he is.

Now, spirits have spoken, and the servant complied and told the daughter that the Holy Spirit had spoken to him to accompany her to the night club; immediately, the Man of God said that to the daughter, and the daughter shouted and jumped up as they arrived at the nightclub. Immediately as the DJ played the music, the daughter called him out to dance with Daddy. Then, as both were dancing, one of the club mates said, look at the Minister of God in the Club dancing with the daughter. The Man of God said he was like to shrink under the ground in that night. Therefore, reader, will you help me to conclude these?

Please, attention here

It says, "A man's heart plans his way, but the Lord directs his steps" (proverbs 16:9); many of the faiths always pray to direct our ways. I mean, when I was a young Christian, any time I wanted to do something, I would always pray with this scripture for direction, but without knowing that it's all proverbs.

So when a man's heart plans, then he directs his steps, so if the spirits are leading our ways as written, that means many of the faith would not be getting problems of life anymore. So for them to direct our steps probably not in the proper ways of our heart's desires. However, Spirits' ways and we understand scriptures define their work as stealing, killing, and destroying.

Tell me, if the director of your ideas is your opposition, how then do we expect that verse of the script above to be profitable in our life?

"A man's steps are of the Lord. How then can man understand his way?" (Proverbs 20:24) I can say many of us the faiths have been carried away and forgotten that mostly all scriptures in the books of proverbs, palms, and Ecclesiastes are all in proverbs and idioms.

For this, the spirits read our inner mind and are also ready to change whatever we are planning to do without our knowledge. Therefore, if our steps are in the hands of the opposition, which we did not know, it all means they will do with us whatever their wish is. Contributed religions are everywhere in the world today, with all kinds of names under the leadership of these spirits.

It says, "The king's heart is in the hand of the Lord, as the rivers of water, he turns it to wherever he wishes." (Proverbs 21: 1)

Before, I used to understand this passage of the scripture, with the meaning that no matter how terrible a man/woman may be, that my Lord will reign over him, and he will show me a favor. However, without the real meaning that the scripture is talking about the faiths mostly. That was also confirmed.

(Revelation 1:6). So it simply means as the spirit reads and understands the inner thoughts of Man and may ready to change it by ministering or whispering to the person concerned something similar to the initial plans, and the person will follow it up. Substitutes are the works of beings.

Please pay attention to this. With experience, if I say to you that a vast percentage of us who borrowed money from the bank and later struggled to make payments are cursed by these spirits.

They are ready to stir/motivate you, and you will be excited to go and borrow or to buy something like goods, houses, cars. Or anything on credit/credit card which they are quite well the person will later find it difficult, or may not even be able, to complete the payment. Very easy in terms of what they can do

The principal works of these beings, the major Problems of the Entire World:

Praying against Satan, stop wasting your time, the Spirits are making fools of you": Uses doctrines to hold right from Pope down to the "Catholic Reverends" not to being involved in marital issues while other religious Ministers were marring, living together with their Families:

Cast mind back to Roman Catholic history and the Church of England or go to the Vatican of Pope in Rome and witness what was built there through religion?
The devil is a liar.

A considerable percentage of us did not understand what these authorities are. I was so lucky that these beings do not quickly kill human beings, at least physically. If not, they would have killed me long ago before I got to know them. As these spirits cannot quickly kill, if they were, most of the mad people seen around should have been dead long ago because the same are the authorities of the madness.

The worst part of it is, if these spirits lowered voice and speak to you, you may decide to give them whatever sum is in your pocket. Due to enticing, appealing, and attractive words, they are also able to communicate with you because they read and understand our minds.

These are the natural beings that are familiar to Man, the authorities of religions; including Idol shrines (traditional beliefs). They are right here on earth with us, monitoring everyone 24hrs, irrespective of faith. These high percentages were not aware of these beings around them, so they are not the spirits of our relatives as some people preach or assume?

For example, they monitor you and me. Following and soaring along with us, without many being aware of Spirits' existence around us. They cannot seem so easy, even while they are around you, and they can reluctantly whisper tremendous or bad things to you, and you will think that your inner mind is talking or whispering to you. Like issues someone may have against you, or what somebody did to you in the past, in a way to cause split if possible and likewise, the other way around and also able to steal the thoughts of your inner mind without you remembering it, these are one of the reasons very many of us were sometimes without memory or most of the time being out of mind.

Sometimes people are behaving unwisely. Mostly in the areas like snatching the country's money to a developed country, terrorising, and suicide bombers: violence attacks, kidnapping etc. These are the key works and the intents of the spirits against the living. It started in the scripture, where Cain killed Abel, and Lamech killed Cain. Also, remember what happened in the US on Septemmber11 2001; Spirits motivate stirred people to act irresponsibly, and these are intents of the beings against the living, but we humans lack a proper understanding of the works of the spirits in our midst.

Three-quarters of today's human's problems, especially in the third world countries are as a result of these beings. For example, people running mad (madness) mostly are caused by these beings. Busy burning fires, a fire, destroying residences, fire burning markets, and destroying fortunes/treasures. That will lead many to poverty road accidents; spirits motivate the driver, mostly the night drivers, to fall asleep at the wheel. Go to African countries and witness what died there through an accident in a year; you will be amazed. These beings mainly cause poverty, Illiteracy, misunderstandings amid relatives, all, and these are the primary things that give them pleasure Ref... (Gen11:7). Says, "Come, let us go down and confuse their languages that they may not understand one another's speech?

The hopeless beings give people Vision and dream at asleep, which may come to pass (probability). Sometimes, it may be to deceive someone by taking their mind out from their target.

Do you know that a good percentage of single women of today that are still hanging around, these beings are caused? Ref... (Isaiah 4:1) says, "On that day; Seven women shall take hold of a man saying, "We will eat our food and wear our apparel, only let us be called by your name, to take away our reproach." These are spirits' ways of mocking humans.

A lady sexily/dreaming having sex in a dream at asleep are caused by the coupled of spirits for so long monitoring the person without her knowledge. These are the significant issues and reasons why they mostly like keeping some ladies for so long before they can get married. Consider these are also the Spirits that say Adam and Eve have sinned in the Garden of Eden.

The critical tricks of the beings before the flocks; they find it reluctantly in directing single ones in the congregation to who their spouse will be. Also, is increasing the number of single ones in today's churches not to get married on time or as scheduled. That is because the spirits are not happy over humans being adequately married.

These beings can change whatever your plans are. Then, you find yourself doing what you are not supposed to be doing without knowing it. These spirits can make you marry somebody, whether you like the person or not, without knowing the reason. Later on, the person will be wondering; it may be somebody who snores at sleep or somebody that has a terrible odour. It is quite natural for the spirits to join both of you together, and the person would be your wife or your husband. Just consider marital systems in churches.

These authorities can also inspire you to marry somebody who is not mannered. In my understanding, they know the positions of every church member. Including their academic, financial, and Family backgrounds. They know

Those who are with reasonable skill and also those who have almost everything that you may have needed. So if eventually both of you get married, within time, people will be amazed. However, they are not ready to join such brethren. Instead, they would like to join people that will keep surviving, and that will make them not to run away from the Church. Remember that never a time will these beings give/allow you to have the exact thing that you may have needed, even in the Church. It's scriptural; examples – are the story of Jacob, Laban, Leah, and Rachael in the bible, but we did not know that.

Familiar spirits can remind you what happened in your family many years ago, even when you forgot about it. They are also able to motivate somebody, and the person will show you favour without you knowing it. Likewise, they can make your Boss, Manager, or even your flat/roommate to develop a dislike for you without reason. Mostly, in marriages, in place of work, line managers, in schools, in the Governments, market place etc.

In a polygamous family, where a man is married to two, they never, ever stand to see the two women living in peace. Also, never holds to see the first son on both sides.

Stand to see each other progress without envy, even in their usual way, unsure one side of the family is doing very well in life more than the opposite. Quote me, in a way to cause hatred and division among them, regardless of their faith.

Greatest Mistake

Further, in a family, parents may sometimes utter a positive or negative word on/to their children, either in anger or when they are happy—depending on what the children in question have done. Sometimes, they could have said to their children that their children would treat them likewise. These words usually come through, but only because the familiar spirits are always there with them. So, people must be careful of the words they speak out at any time since they are still within to use whatever they say to work against their fellow humans. The spirits can keep a record for many, many years without forgetting it.

In 1999, by the time we were passing through the wilderness, for the sake of the false promise that was made to me in our local Church by these authorities. That's why the testing of the trial takes place, and along the line, all their tricks are discovered because of unfulfilled, and it happened one morning, as I came back from my night job around 5:45 am, and without delay, I made up my mind and drove off to the morning prayer in my Church. After we had finished, I picked up my car and ran home. As I stepped into my sitting room and knelt to pray and give thanks for the day, I became fragile, and on my knee there, I fell asleep. Well, I do not know how I managed to find myself in the bed inside my bedroom. I hope you have not forgotten that at this time of the tribulation. These spirits increased much in number, monitoring me all around. Even while in my local Church. Just for the sake of the trail of the promised, ref. The children of Israel tested, even Jesus. So, whenever there is a promise from these authorities, the testing will take place.

So, as I found myself in the bed, I could see myself dreaming and having perfect sex with what I could not be able to describe. No matter the spirits intention, because I was very prayerful at that time. Though, before I realised and got up, I had already messed myself up with sperm.

I got up and quietly looked around the bedroom, surprisingly. I noticed all these beings within my bedroom and did not know what to do. Then I stood, felt shy, offended God, you know, as a born-again Christian. I knelt praying to pardon me, for that was the cause of the devils.

So, what I'm trying to let us know is that every sex human being has in the dream is caused by those familiar spirits monitoring a name for ages. Not a different one, and these types of things mainly happened because of not having a sexual relationship for a while.

As a Christian and as human Nature, sometimes, the person concerned will be feeling somehow sexy, and those spirits are around, reasoning his/her mind.

That is why while the person is asleep, these spirits will help/motivate the person in their usual way to be in a deep sleep while these spirits will cling on the person's clothes and private parts. Mostly, women, the spirits will be mingling themselves together as if swimming. While these spirits will be doing that, the person will be feeling it even in a better way than having sex with a natural human being, likewise to men.

However, they are likely to get women more quickly than men due to the Nature of their private parts. Some of those spirits will be on the person's face, helping the person to sleep very well and at the same time giving visions and dreams so that the person will keep dreaming about It, and also in a way not to let the person wake up until those spirits are satisfied.

Therefore, if you are experiencing such, all you need is awareness of the beings around you 24hrs. They have nothing good for you and are there for your downfall. If they noticed that you recognise their presence, those beings would stop troubling you in that area, no matter how long they have been doing it, because they hate to be exposed.

The World may have been deceived for ages by these spirits, but their end has come.

I could remember years back that one of our family members, who was a practising Catholic, went to marry a lady in C.M.S. After this young Man had proposed to the Sister, both families agreed together. Eventually, the Sister discovered that the young Man's family was not a C.M.S. Member. Could you believe it?

That the marriage could not hold because the young Man's family is not a C.M.S. church member. This Sister was so selective, and this kept her from marrying until she was 45 years of age. You may now say she lacks understanding. Many Christians at that time could not marry on time. Some of them married in their Old age. Just because if you were from another church, they would ask why not join our Church, and then we would be able to marry each other.

However, today, people have come to their senses and also marry from other faiths.

A further example: back home in Africa; it happened that I was into a relationship with a lady, and both of us have been involved for a couple of years then, and it happened. I lived afar off, and she lives in the eastern part of the country. Sometimes both of us will not see each other for a couples of months, due to the Nature of our job. So, as I visited her one day, she narrated to me how she saw herself in a dream of having sex with me. She thought it was a real situation, not knowing it was a dream.

When she woke up, she saw that she had wet herself, which made her annoyed. On the next time/day of my visit, while I was lying in bed with her discussing, I did not know how I managed to pick up her small bible because she was a partial Catholic then. As I opened the guide, it was like something stirred /said to me to read this, while both of us were not yet real Christians then. That was somewhere in the book of (Hebrew13:4) that says, "Marriage is honourable, among all bed undefiled, fornication and adultery will judge. "So, immediately I closed that very chapter because of any discussion about marriage as of that time was not possible.

So, my dear, I do not know what was the reasons. Any time the lady will bring/raise the issues of marriage, I always ignored them, as we love ourselves so much that one can think of, so after this great discovery, I realised all the tricks of these spirits against the singles. Could you imagine the cunning manipulation of them? Working against us all these while, that's the lady so dear and should have been somebody I supposed gotten married to even before I left the country. Then, because of unforeseen circumstances around us, that was not possible. Therefore, if you are experiencing such, all you need is awareness of the beings around you 24hrs. They have nothing good for you and are there for your downfall. If they noticed that you recognise their presence, those beings would stop troubling you in that area, and no matter how long they have been doing it, because they hate to be exposed. The World may have been deceived for ages by these spirits, but their end has come.

The wickedness of the beings: our eyes, ears and mind needs awareness of the beings around us 24hrs:

Sometimes, when we mention the spirits, many of us assume spirits in human forms due to the way some people witness them in a vision or dream. Even though they follow and monitor everyone at all times, without recognition of their presence, not talk about what they can do. As little as they are, even among servants of the gospels. Well, I will say that a lot of us even the non-religious, have seen the spirits. Without recognizing that they are the beings we talk about, which are also the devils (natural ancestral/familiar). They are at all times, follow and monitor us due to the height of their wickedness and their jealousy over us.

Again, sometimes, many of us misunderstand the ways they show up in their wickedness. That sometimes results in every bad thing that happens to us being regarded that the devil's cause. However, as the author, I'm here to announce us, mostly, the wickedness of the beings is not by any means but through what they have ministered/whispered to you or through anyone associating with you. Or using someone around to achieve their aims. These are also the ways they have been ministering to ministers. So, there is never a time they will do any of their tricks against us without through whispering or motivating, whether positively or negatively. So, whatever they are about to do us, they likely using somebody around us or ministering/

whispering to you or me as a person and you will think your inner mind is doing it. Remember what happened in the stories between Adam and Eve, with the serpent in the Garden of Eden.

So, in reality, their plan here on Earth is to steal, kill, and to destroy as it's written. Now, with these ideas, you can see that none of the three things that define their works is profitable to Man. You can also see that the faiths (the

Entire World) have for thousands of ages been fooling in the hands of nonentity beings, and they are not bothered due to their evil Nature.

Nevertheless, as their tricks have discovered, ministers of the gospels, those who are from time to time receiving messages/instructions from them, will, from now on, keep watching how they will reluctantly be speaking because ignorance is their Nature. On the other hand, if I want to define the three works of the beings against us, probably. I will say to steal equally means, not by any other way, but through taking in these various areas. In our finances, our inner thoughts, our visions, and dreams.

Mostly before the congregations, they will be doing that through the preaching and teaching of the words. The faiths will be putting in the house; with the hope the authorities will be giving back as written. In the book of (Luke 6:38), It says "Give, and it shall be given back unto you, good measure pressed down shaken together and running over, will be put into your bosom, for with the same measure that you use, it measured back to you", but my question is this, is it true? Because many have emptied their pockets in the

Church, etc., without receiving any tangible rewards, look at all the Church building, etc., in the Entire World. Mostly in third world countries, where the societies or Church do not get support from the Government for building Churches.

All were constructed through contributions of men and women of these ages or have you seen the bible creator send money from sky/heaven to the representatives? So, all these are done through stealing from the congregations through the preaching and teaching of the words.

24HRS AWARENESS

Another trick we would like to share is stealing from us. Let me give you another example of the tricks of stealing. In the year 2001, in London, England, during the cause/wilderness on which the Spirits discovered to be otherwise. On one of the nights, a vision of Ashibornern (Christian Prayer Centre) shown to me. Still, I did not understand the idea well. After 2days, they also gave me a couple of scriptures for the same purpose. That helps to make it clear to me that the Lord wanted me to go on outing prayer to a place called Ashibornern outside London. However, I was so disturbed because, during this time in my wilderness, I struggled to feed myself, let alone have some money on me for any other thing. Still, I later went for the outing prayer for a couple of weeks. I think that surely, the Lord will use it to bring the wilderness to an end by the time I finish the prayer. I almost borrowed money for my return.

Well, being human after the prayer in the year 2001, and looking forward to something good to happen was when all my problems seemed to increase. I do not know if you understand what I have said here.

So, I later started reasoning and asked myself, what then was the purpose of that outing prayer? Then, not knowing that the beings used that way to empty (steal) the little money I had on me. Remember, during this time in the wilderness, their tricks have not yet been discovered. Also, mind you that there will never be a time the beings will put hands into your pocket and take whatever you have there. Still, through one way or the other, they will motivate/stir you up, and you will do that yourself.

Another way of stealing I would like to share with us is this;

In London, Life Newspaper of Monday, March 10, 2008, Page 17 had an article that said, "Modern-day Moses' faces jail for £3.2m church theft. University dropout, 24, preyed

On 1,000 worshippers, a "Modern-day Moses" who fleeced churchgoers out of more than£3.2m faces jail today. Lindani Mangena, 24, preyed on over 1,000 worshippers in Seventh-Day Adventist congregations in London to feed his appetite for luxury. Mangena posed as a city trader to convince them to invest in a bogus spread–betting formula. Southwark Crown Court heard that, along with two accomplices, he promised profits of up to 3,000 percent in six months. Many victims, including widows and pensioners, were forced to re-mortgage their homes—much of their money spent on property cars and holidays. One hotel stays in Dubai cost £55,815.

Building surveyor Desmond Vincent, who lost £70,000 and even quit his job to try to work for Magana, told the court, "We thought he was like a modern-day Moses. I thought the Lord had blessed him. Now he could not sell me chewing gum." Mangena, 24, of Maidstone Avenue, Romford, was found guilty of fraudulent trading, money laundering, and carrying on unauthorised investment business. Dean Hinkson,29 of Bensham Lane, West Corydon, and Curtis Powell, 31 of Hythe Road, Thornton Heath were convicted of communicating an investigation or inducement to engage in investment activity. Today's victim, Lucy Acquah, a council worker, told she was swindled out of £76,000 after re-mortgaging her home and using money set aside for her sons' education for the get richQuick scheme. A 49-year-old mother of four, from Norbury said, "I lost a lot. I could not put my sons through their education, so I feel like a failure." I have been furious about this, but sending Lindani to prison does not resolve the problem. I want my money back. "When I went to see him in 2003, he had an impressive office near the Bank of England. He convinced me that I would receive £35,000 a profit. A year later, there was just an answering phone message saying the company was undergoing restructuring." Only a fraction of the cash received was invested, while the gang used the rest to fund a life of luxury. Mangena, a university dropout, even laid down deposits on a £4.8m penthouse at St George Wharf. All three men will be sentenced today and told it is inevitable. DC Mel Moody of the City of London Police Fraud Squad said, "Mangena targeted those he knew had. Little or no knowledge of financial matters. He heartlessly used religion to defraud victims out of every penny he could.

"You may now ask; how does it happen in the Church of living God? But I'm here to announce to you, so far, these spirits are concerned, nothing is impossible to happen in the Church because the spirits heading the churches are unusual beings mind you, these doses not happened in less than one year. Plus, you also know that for the Church to have up to 1,000 members, it will take a couple of years.

These were discovered but not because spirits revealed them but after the promise has not been fulfilled. Due to tricks of the authorities leading the Church, certain things will be getting out of hand in the Church without specifics instruction to the Minister. Even if the Pastor was not initially informed, the authorities were supposed to have revealed it to the Minister before it was exposed. Or, will you convince me, that the spirits were unaware, well that's also parts of stealing of them from the congregations? Because, initially, the victims (brethren) trusted God without given it a second thought.

In the Newspaper one Nigeria armed robber called (holy robbers) alias babe as published in Nigeria Weekly Spectator. July 2, 2006. Page35 Crime World.

Fasts and pray before the operation.

Greatest Mistake

A commercial bus driver who the police described as ferocious stunned. Detectives are interrogating him recently when he said that he used to go to churches and mosques for individual prayer and fasting sessions before going out for an operation in Lagos.

Its environs. Biodun Akinbawa, alias Babeke, gave a graphic account of how his gang operated before it fell to the superior firepower of men of the anti-robber squad from Pedro Police Station in Shomolu, Lagos. Nigeria.

Babeke, as the career criminal fondly called, told Weekly Spectator, Yes, I am a robber but not an armed one. I only used my bare hands to torture my victims, and that is only when they disobeyed my orders. Nevertheless, if the passengers complied with my orders, my gang members would not harm them. He further revealed that before he goes for any robbery operation. He usually goes to mosques or churches to pray and sometimes fast. Although he is a free thinker, he said, "I do not discriminate against religions.

I can go to any mosque today, and the following day, I can go to any church. I do not' belong to any sect." Continuing, he said, "I believe that we are serving the same creator, call him Allah, call him Jesus or Yahweh. He is the same. I believe in the power of prayer to God. I do not visit native doctors because I know that their powers of worship to God are limited." On whether God answers his prayers or not during operations, he said, "It is difficult to understand."

He said that he joined the evil gang through a friend he met in an Indian hemp/cocaine joint. He told me that if I followed him to rob, I would get money to open up a big shop. Then I could stop. However, see what is happening to me now. I did not make money, yet I am facing the worst disgrace on earth. He lamented. He was giving a blow-by-blow account of how the gang operated. He said that they used to pick up unsuspected passengers from the Ojota bus stop, and along the route, they would dispossess them of their money, mobile phones, and other valuables. He revealed that after dispossessing the passengers of their belongings. They would push them out of the bus one by one at different locations and then turn back to pick up other passengers. On how they dealt with stubborn passengers, he said, "Who are you to cough when you see seven wild-looking men like us?" Once we shout at our victims, they become afraid instantly; you know Lagosians fear for their lives a lot. They love their lives. So they do not argue with us. It was only once that one boy tried to play smart with us, and we gave him the beating of his life.

However, the state police spokesman, Olabode Ojajuni, described Babeke as a "furious armed robber" who had tortured many of his victims.

Luck ran out on him when the police caught him and members of the gang while they were robbing people.

Well, hopefully, I do not think we need further explanations about churches and mosques being a place of refuge for armed robbers in the country of Nigeria and some others. All these sometimes result because these countries are in the wilderness with the spirits. Governments seem inferior in every aspect. As I have mentioned before about their tricks in the churches and mosques, etc., you may witness that the example of robbers given may be the least of robber's ways of operation in most of the African countries, to the extent of what is happening there. Mind you, the robbers' victims, many of them have been born-again Christians.

Who must have prayed before going out for various daily needs? Along the line, they fall into armed robbers. Well, it's not a strange story. It seems to be a custom, and you, too know quite well. These types of group robbers did not start out of the blue or two years ago; that must have been their occupation right from time immemorial. At the same time, that's also their usual way of praying in churches and mosques all this time. They have been destroying people. These guys must have been under 45 years. I hope you know what it means? It is only a fool who will say their prayers made them caught this time. Just help me conclude that concerning how the spirits operate in churches, mosques, etc.

Remember the scripture in (Isaiah 54:17) says, "No weapon formed against you shall prosper, and every tongue which rises against you in judgment you shall condemn." Nevertheless, the question is this. Is that true? Is that verse of scripture valid, and they dupe brethren before the eyes of the Holy Ghost; you need to answer this question for your reader(s).

Another way of stealing from us is in the area of our thoughts, visions, and dreams, which are even more dangerous than others. These are the reasons that they are monitoring every single person day and night. However, mind you that this can be possible depending on an individual; the scriptures say if you can believe, then it will happen to you. That means if you accept whatever you have ministered/whispered, that's it. They are always there with us, especially during times of difficulties.

Whenever people are in a difficult situation, hardship, and problem, struggling in the things of life, that is the time the beings that monitor us will show up, even ready to invite others spirits within to help reluctantly and mess the person's mind up. With all kinds of suggestions in a way to divert attention to something lower than what you needed in that very situation. These are the reasons you will mostly find people end up in churches with all kinds of problems, just because of what the beings have done through negative suggestions. Then, people find themselves regretting and end up in different sects of religions. These days, it is challenging to get up to 3% of people to decide to go to church for the sake of making it into Heaven after death. Many have forgotten their visions in life and went into the ministry, and they used them to achieve their arms. Some were favoured, and some are not. Also, many have been diverted or stolen by the beings from their initial plans. They found themselves doing something different without knowing the cause; this stealing was found in the area of marriage and business, where many have gone into marriages because of what the beings have said through the Ministers/Church Elders.

Well, the most crucial thing I would like us to discern is that the spirit's works, which are to steal, kill, and to destroy, have nothing suitable for humanity. Some Ministers are favoured today, and not because they love their servants most. Still, they have no other choice and ways of getting attention and achieving their trade, so they must use human beings to get it done.

Right from the time I came out from this wilderness, I noticed one thing that some unbelievers seem to have firm faith, ever more than the real Christians, without minding all their lifestyles. Believers have suffered to the point of asking where our King is. Even to the point, some third-world countries do not realize or know that they are suffering anymore because it has become part of our lives.

So, my dear, it is time to start writing petitions to advanced governments about this, to find ways of kicking out the opposed (Ancestral/Familiar) spirits from our midst because they are the obstacles behind the growth of our individual and countries' economies. Without that, we will still be beating around the bush; I do not know if you understand that the beings are experts in attacking the country's economy by using those without value in the government's authority. For example, look at the present stands of all the nations that are known for their religions in third-world countries.

I mean, the undeveloped countries that have devoted themselves so much to these authorities. The economy of these countries has been the target of these beings because they are yielding to these beings. For example, how many of these independent modern churches in Nigeria, Ghana, Sierra Leone, etc., are established by a white skin brother if there is no deception in religions? If at all there are any, how many are there? Look at all the modern churches that are in America, Britain, and Germany, etc., they are all mostly established by Nigerians, Ghanaians, and Sierra Leoneans, why?

Because of one thing or the other, they are mostly giving attention to these beings, and the spirits have no option other than to speak and use us to do their work. According to the scripture, the entire world is called to spread the word, not just only Africans. In the early Christian era, westerners brought missionaries to Africa. However, today, Africans have taken over, and not because we have a better understanding of the written words. So, just think about it and today, Westerners who thought of third-world country's religion have now decided to go to church only on Christmas, Easter, and in their old age because they find no tangible thing in religion.

Honestly, the beings we are talking about are more than what we can imagine in times of deception. Remember, the same spirits always bring temptation around us to help and draw our attention to the church. Too many of us have held down for so long, mostly in third-world countries. By praying, fasting, and depending on these authorities to bring miracles across our paths. Without putting actions into our situations. Whenever they see that you are struggling to survive, they will do all they can for you to end up there, even among the congregation. No one will question. That's the reason why beings capitalize or get the most out of us by using mainly black to achieve their business.

Many of us are still struggling due to our weak economy and poor government management. Look at most countries in the Western world. They have used their forefathers in the past to bring missionaries to most third-world countries. However, at present, because of their wealth. There is nothing that they can use to attract the majority of them anymore because they have gotten almost what they wanted; now, they get revenge because the spirit never let go, and as we know, ignorance is their nature, causing problems in their marriages.

That is the main reason many of them do not think about religion anymore, and there is nothing that the beings can do about it other than start using the blacks that are giving them attention.

For example, look at the life of some gospel Ministers, who had seven or eight branches or more in different parts of the world. In each of these churches, the general overseer will ordain someone to Pastor a Church under the basis of remuneration, preachers. Everyone is aware of this that some Ministers have many branches, which means having a church is an excellent investment; why? Because the authorities are a spirit of strategies, tricks, and manipulation, every minister is supposed to be entitled to one church to take proper care of the congregation. You will find out that those ministers with many branches have not gotten enough time for others. Because they maintain constant visits to all the departments from time to time and while they are doing that, they will have less time to see people in any of these branches.

The beings, be who they are in the area of deception, keep quiet over these. Those Ministers with many branches are very easy to locate, and there exist different kinds of slip-ups in them. I hope you know that because a Minister has many offices to attend to, he will now have very little time for a single branch within the group, and his overall performance will, therefore, swing to a decline.

A further example of the other works of these authorities here on Earth is to kill. Many will ask, how do they do that? The answer is straightforward, though. I hope you still remember that there is never a time that they will kill physically; and instead, they use people. Now you can see that in the three things that define their works, none of their achievements were done without the use of people; even the person or those groups of people they are using will never understand what is behind their doing.

Examples, at the time of this writing, in my place of work and through my flatmate in London, England. They have used/motivated people to inject poison in my food for me to perish so that the writing of their exposure will come to an end. Also, both are women, though their efforts were discovered.

Most importantly, the easiest way they kill people is through gunmen (armed robbers), road accidents, and a plane crash. Just by making/motivating the pilot (driver) to fall asleep at the wheel, this is easy as a b c, as far as the beings are concerned.

Another way that they use people to kill is through bombing; through suicide bombers, many have lost their lives here on earth, and this is what they can do in terms of killing, cast your mind back to the set of fire on human beings in South African recently, that what it is.

Then, the third work of beings is to destroy. Destruction is one of the easiest ways that they use to get Families, whole tribes, or individuals down. I mean, their most comfortable way to make people useless in life without achieving anything. Also, I appreciate the way they tried to put me during and after this wilderness. They have never for one day stopped trying to get me down by attacking my finances and discouragement, for them not to be exposed, to witness to you how brutal and hopeless they are. These are the things that helped me so much to discover all the ways of their operations. I'm sure you know that they use people to destroy their fellow humans in several ways,

URGENT ATTENTION, SINGLES

Just to witness to us the way spirits manipulate the singles irrespective of faith. Here is one of the most known spirit tricks against the single ones in their marriage. These things happened to me a couple of times in my local church where I worship — by that time, looking for who cared to settle down when I had not noticed the intention of these authorities for the wilderness. It happened as I proposed to a very lovely sister, and after praying for a couple of months, she told me that her mind did not accept the proposal. Then, after some time, the sister showed up, but by that time, even though still looking around, my mind had waxed cool against her.

Did you know? Right from that very year, the Lord promised to give me a life partner in the church where

I worship. And after a couple of months, the very same sister was also shown to me, living together with me — as a couple, and she was carrying a baby boy with her. I asked her what was wrong with the baby because the child was crying in that vision, and she responded that nothing serious was wrong with the baby. This happened in the year 1998, during the beginning of the wilderness. That very sister shown to me as my wife by the spirits was also the very sister that I mentioned in these volumes that her family consulted the police to advise me with the message that the sister was not my wife.

So, what I want you to identify is this. As I proposed to the sister, spirits kept her mind cool, which made her not accept my proposal. When these authorities opened her heart to accept the proposal, the same powers kept my mind cool against the sister, making me lose interest. These happened between me and two other sisters in my local church. For reasons, spirits will not allow me to settle down until after the wilderness; that's a trick used against many singles in marital issues, irrespective of faith. Reference (*Proverbs*21:1) The king's heart is in the hand of the Lord; like the rivers of water he turns wherever he wishes. Also, God said to Moses I would harden the heart of Pharaoh.

Urgent Attention Singles
Too many singles have encountered the same problem without reason.

A similar one to the one above happened to a dear brother in the Lord. Also, a workmate with a calling from God in his life, this is the guy the spirits used to bring me into the modern church. So, as both of us were working at the same company and at the same time worshipping in the same church, it happened as this brother wanted to settle down before answering the calling of God into the ministry.

Then, the brother proposed to a lovely, well-educated sister in the same church. After that, both started dating and praying over it. As time passed, the sister would visit us at our workplace at Knightsbridge West End London during the dating intervals. After discussing and charting, the sister left. So, as they were doing this for three months, and by the end of the third month, the sister replied that her mind did not accept the proposal; the brother was shocked. It is really unbelievable because both of us banks hope for her. Even the sister is more interested because the brother has a calling from God in to the ministry in his life. I mean, the brother is almost a minister. Then, after one year, another sister was confirmed to the brother by the church authorities, though the brother had no choice but to accept the sister as his wife; within some months, they wedded, and as time goes the lady conceived, unfortunately, after giving birth to two, the sister died within 8 to 9 years in her marital life.

Listen, the sister that replied and said her mind did not welcome the proposal. The sister did not understand what was behind what she did. Had she known, the brother would have been the right person for her because both love each other, which one can use as a reference/compliment. The authorities of religion, I mean, the spirits guiding the church, would never have allowed you to get exactly what you wanted, in steady will give you somebody that two of you will keep surviving in a way to keep the focus on him and church activities. I suppose I have mentioned this before.

The most dangerous tricks of the spirits against me after coming out from the wilderness. But this time, the spirits' tricks have been discovered. It happened as I came out from the terrible wilderness. I started looking for a job, going from one to another. One day, with luck, I discovered a family bakery owned by a Jamaican in Cold Harbour Lane, Brixton area of London. After having been employed, it was like hell had broken loose. Those spirits monitoring me could not believe it.

Why? Because, at that time, not have my stand in the UK, I was still employed, and also, they were not happy with me for discovering their tricks and looking for ways to make a note out of it. I don't know if you really catch the point.

Ministers and those with spiritual understanding will be able to catch my points and what I went through. Do not forget that after discovering tricks, spirits in high numbers monitored me. Some clung all over my clothes even whilst working in the bakery, and we were about 20 to 25 workers there. Still, spirits did not bother — just to witness the height of their stubbornness, selfishness, and wickedness.

As you know, I will not let my employer and co-workers understand what I am going through; instead, I will be sacked.

Urgent Attention, Singles

Remember, as spirits monitor, it is not personal, so my employers and other workers are also being monitored by the same familiar spirits; confidence you still remember how it was explained how spirits move information within them? Therefore, immediately, I stepped into the family bakery looking for a Job; all the spirits monitored everyone there and were aware of whom I was and my intention; nothing was hidden before them. As time goes on in the bakery job, as you know, spirits are never in a hurry doing things.

My only saviour in that job was on the day I was employed, the very owner of the company (senior director) was there, the first son to the director was there, Married and most senior daughter, single parent of the man was there, well-educated, the son of the director is the employment manager and the most senior daughter manager both seemed to manage the business for their daddy. Do not forget; this is outside my church's families because right from the day tricks was discovered between 2003 to 2005, had never for one day stepped into any church again even though since then, spirits had never for one day stopped clinging all over my clothes day and night for intimidation.

I am expressing these just to witness to us spirit tricks strategists with confidence that people in a similar situation will be delivered. So, right from the day I was employed, the spirits were doing their best to see that I was sacked. I do not need to tell you this; you are supposed to know this. After working with them for the past three to four years, they all like me because I work with all my heart as a born-again Christian, the director, the son, and the daughter. It happened as the families witnessed my loyalty to the job and the entire family. The spirits stir the daughter, the manager, up to eyeing me for marriage, and by this time, I have been working with them for six to seven years. Do not forget that all along, both in the church and after the wilderness, I have been going from one end to the other, looking for somebody to settle down with. The same spirits blocking it because if I have settled down, I will now have the got to write and expose them.

Therefore, the lady, a Jamaican British-born, my manager in her father's factory, spirits stirred her to eye me for marriage, and the entire family was aware. How do you reason it? This is a lady with master's degree certificates who is driving and paying her mortgage. I mean, she has all I need. So, the lady was doing all she could for her intention to happen. But to be honest with you, even though I so like the lady, because she is very hardworking and very sensible. But my mind did not accept her intention. I mean, spirits so block my entire mind not to accept her, even though I have come out from the wilderness and understood all their tricks, just to witness the power of spirits if they decide to seize someone's mind. "The king's heart is in the hand of the Lord; like the rivers of water, he turns wherever he wishes." *(Proverbs 21:1)*

As the lady clearly understood that her intention would not work out, one day, she spoke to my hearing that she would screw me out of this factory. Well, there was nothing I could do; my mind was so blocked against her, and after doing her best to red-card me from the factory, that did not work out because there was no way she would terminate my job without the consent of the employment manager and their daddy. And the employment manager and their daddy are so much like me, and how I put every effort into working for them. Now, as her plan failed, she started cutting my wages. Now, when the wife (manager) of the employment manager joined the company, one day, she called me into the office and said to me that for a while, I have been paying lower wages and that from today/week, she will increase my wages from 230 pounce to 260 pay per week, confidence your following, and this is my eight to nine years working in that family bakery. Now, one day, when she was on holiday to Jamaica and came back, there was a kind of suspected movement she made toward my locker in the factor; from that day, I decided to leave that family bakery for another even though I have not gotten my stand in the UK, and by that time have worked with them for ten years. One day, I called the employment manager and told him that I had stopped working in two weeks, and that was how I vacated the job.

Points to consider?

I was 36 years old when I joined the church, looking for someone to settle down with, and after one year, the wilderness started. Throughout all these times, they have not allowed me to get somebody. Therefore, how, then, do you think the same spirits will allow me to settle down with my director's daughter?

Be careful here; the spirits have done all they can for me to lose the bakery job, but no way. Then, they diverted, stirring the lady to be eyeing me for marriage and, at the same time, hardening my heart for her intention, for the lady, because of that, to terminate my job; I hope you're getting the points. Their plans against me in that job also showed us that not everything spirits can do. If not, I should have one way or the other lost that job in under one year because I had no stand in the UK. Still, I was there with complete obedience for a good 10 years. I am so lucky that the employment manager and their daddy were so wonderful. I mean, people to use as a reference, which is why the lady cannot sack me without their approval. If not, the spirits should have used the lady to terminate my job in under one year, and the lady would never understand what was behind her doing. Moreover, the spiritual understanding I have so much helped me to stand the attacks of the spirits in that job for ten years. Only those with spiritual understanding will understand my points here.

If I ask you, where can we find those spirits stirrings the lady all this while? Listen carefully. The Bible says that your body is the temple of the holy ghost, mind you, not inside your body, because anything that enters inside your stomach dies instantly. But outside your body, in the hairs of your head, look, human hairs are likening to green glass where spirits lay eggs, as I mentioned somewhere in these books before, and on the very clothes you wear at that moment. So, as the spirits breathe out, that air will enter inside you the same way air wind goes inside humans. As they do that, the person involved will feel uncomfortable. If you want them to keep off on you, then you need to do something about it.

Firstly, let them understand that now you are aware of whatever fuck they are doing in your life. I assured you immediately they know that now you understand their tricks, in good conscience, they will keep off on you, and do your best to meditate on their tricks day and night on how spirits act and manipulate people here and there. They will wholeheartedly depart from you once they notice you are thinking about them regularly. You're now very dangerous to them because they will not like you making it known to a third party.

Similar Tricks. And Me
Last Attempts.

These last few times, as I have gained my stand in the UK, in the very estate where I live, it happened one day as I was coming back from work, there is a passage in that same building that I needed to go over before I get to my house door. And in that passage, there are other flats before mine; so, it happened as I was coming back from work, a lady, black British, a single mum and new tenant in that very building, came out from their apartment with the Mum and stood at their doorstep; as I was passing by to get to my flat door, they greeted me, and with pleasure, I responded, welcomed them for their new apartment and passed over to my flat door.

After that day, on the Friday of the same week, the lady alone repeated it as I was coming back from work; I wore work clothes hi-vis up and down and had some food stuff I bought for the weekend; she stood at her doorstep, as I am passing by to my flat door I met her, we greeted, somehow, she gazes on my attire and the foodstuff I bought without uttering a word. Later, by reasoning with her, I understood that the lady had since they moved into their new apartment for a couple of days, been watching me through her window anytime am coming back from work and believed that I was single and living alone without my knowledge.

Then, on the Saturday of the same week, whilst in the kitchen cooking because I don't work on the weekend, the lady knocked on my door. As I came out and stood with her at the doorstep, she desperately pleaded with me to come and assist her in hanging her telly on the wall. Well, I told her I was busy cooking, even though I don't know how to do that, but I would call a friend who can do that for her, but you will give him something after that. She said okay, that is fine and asked, can I call the guy now, I said okay, I will, just give me some time. Then she said that she was home and I should let her know when the guy was around, and I said okay, fine. Then, after 20 minutes, I called the guy, and he came with some tools; then, I took the guy to the lady. As I knocked on her door, she came out and opened the door and asked us to come inside. As we entered the house, her Mum was in the sitting room, and she welcomed us.

It happened as the guy was about to start hanging the telly. Unfortunately, the guy did not come with the right tools and did not have the right tools to turn the telly. So, as we all discussed and looked for alternatives, I remembered one of my friends who could do that better with Drain. The lady pleaded with me to talk to the second guy that without watching the telly at home, everyone would be feeling reckless. She requested my phone number, and we exchanged phone numbers. She gave me her phone number and the phone number of the Mum in case, and then I promised to call the guy the next Sunday. On Sunday around 10:30 am, the lady called my phone and asked me about the guy, saying that she would go out soon and I sent a text message to her and said to her that I had talked with the guy and that he would be here soon, but mind you, after having hung the telly for you, you will pay him. She replied to the text and said.

Hi, Cy. Aww, thank you so much. I appreciate it; things are tight now as I am not at work. I understand it again. Thank you. Then, as the guy came, I took him to the lady, and we all (and the Mum) were there for over two hours. Luckily, the guy hung two different tellies for her. So, after that, the lady paid 40 pounds for the wages, and the guy accepted with thanks. After discussing and charting, we departed.

Do not forget that I explain these just to witness how the spirits set traps if they decide to fool someone. On Sunday of the same week, whilst in our sitting room writing, the lady gazed through the kitchen window and noticed that I was around; she called my number. Unfortunately, I didn't hear it because I was busy writing, and my music was on; then she knocked on the door. I had it, and as I came out, she asked me to help her with litter to lighten up her cigar, and I responded. After having lit her cigarettes, we stood there for over 30 minutes at the passage, discussing charts before she departed.

Again, did you know right from the day she noticed that I am independent any time she went out with her car and came back, whether I was indoors or not, she parked her car exactly opposite the window of my room, whilst she had parking space opposites the window of her apartment.

So, being human, due to the way she looked very loyal and homely to me since we knew each other, I started imaging how spirits allowed her to come to me so freely, which never happened since I have been looking for a life partner coupled with spirit's tricks were discovered, sometimes. I started thinking of her, and now I have gotten my stand in the UK. If not, I have stopped looking for a life partner until my books are published due to what the spirits were doing all these while settling down and coupled with the pressures of my marriage from my Mum. Now, I made a decision to propose to her. Firstly, I sent her a text message with the words below. Baby, greetings. How far? How are you doing? Are you cooking? I hope you still took your

Urgent Attention, Singles

little girl to school, as you stated yesterday? Have the guys fixed the internet, or are they still coming to you?

As you know, I am at work in Bishopsgate Liverpool Street. Anyway, baby, as you know, I like you and will be happy seeing your face every day. Reader, did you know that the devils showed up immediately after I sent the text to her? From that day, she started parking her car opposite her flat window and stopped parking her car opposite my window. Right from that day, anytime she passed through my window, she would throw away her face on the other side to not see her face, which went on for two weeks.

After a few days, I sent her another text with the words, good morning dear; I hope all is well with everyone in the house. I can figure out your Mum is around and would like to come and see her in the afternoon. Anyway, baby, could you imagine? Immediately, she got that text asking for her Mum, and without delay, she picked her up, went and dropped her at her house, and came back. So, as I was busy doing something inside, she dropped the Mum without my knowledge. Then, before I went to see them, Mum was already gone. Still, I knocked on their door, and the lady came out as both stood at their doorstep charting. I asked her Mum, and she replied she was gone. I was surprised, whilst at the doorstep charting with her, and I called her name and asked her will you marry me so that we live together with your children? She furiously didn't even allow me to finish. She said no. I asked her again, do you want to think about it, but she didn't allow me to finish. She angrily said no, and within minutes, she closed her door and went inside her flat.

Then, the week before that week, her car wasn't anywhere to be found in the yard on Wednesday to Thursday nights. On Friday of the same week, as I came back from work around 6:30 pm, she was not back yet, so I decided to text her and find out where about.

URGENT ATTENTION SINGLES

THE LAST TEXT MESSAGE SENT TO HER

Dear, this is me, CY. What has been going on for two to three days now? I can't see your car in the yard. I hope all is well with you and the children? Again, please cast your mind back to the seven pages of the book outlines left with you to go through how spirits attack, control, and deceive people of the World, which I intend to publish this summer. I may know what you're going through right now. That is why I left the outlines with you for meditation. Knowing you will be attacked when I reveal my intentions to you. That's why you see confusion within you; those spirits are behind it, and I have what it takes to kill them. Yes, I can kill them. That's why they don't want you to get closer to me; they are afraid of me because I know how they operate, and that's what my books talk about. Do you need someone to tell you that the devils are attacking your marriage?

Stirring you up to be driving up and down all the time with your children. Please try to reason? Well, I just decided to text you; if I don't, that means I do not care about you.

Please, there are parcels/deliveries for you in our flat; you can send your boy to come and pick them up.

Could you imagine, on that Friday, after having sent the text message to her around 12noon, she came back with the children and the Mum; after 20 minutes of their arrival in the yard, the Mum knocked on our door, and I came out. I handed their delivery over to her, and she left. Then, around 11:30 pm, two policemen came to our flat and mentioned my name and that they wanted to see me; one of my flatmates came and called me whilst asleep. I woke up and encountered them, and after giving them my details, they said that a lady called them complaining that I was knocking on her door and texting her that if that's true, I should stop it from that day. They said if I didn't comply and the lady called them again, they would not be happy with me; well, I said, "Okay, I had heard what you said and promised to comply," and they left.

Can you believe it? After two days, the police visited me, and the lady started all over again, parking her car opposite the window of my room whilst having a lot of space opposite her own window?

Further Points to Consider:

Only those with spiritual understanding will be able to understand my points here. The character of the spirits is this: At the start, the spirits just stirred the lady up to come to me freely without reservation to use her waste my time and mess my mind up at the end. A scripture verse says who will say, and it comes to pass if the Lord has not commanded it.

Even a kid is aware that a single mother has been looking for a man to father her children for so long. So, not that the lady is not very well interested, she is interested even more than I am in her. Only the car she always parked opposite my window has said all about how her heart is to me. Still, unforeseen circumstances behind her control could not allow her to make a real move. Therefore, even though she called the police for me, which I know is not intentional, there is something behind it, so that means nothing to me; if I had been convicted of living with her and fathering her children, how much more I cannot endure that for her, If not. that equally means I cannot be able to cope with her in our marriage Now, let me say this again, a Pastor says if he preaches. If you feel uncomfortable, that means you're affected, then you need to repent, do something about it, to avoid repetitions, and find a solution to it for that problem to be solved.

Did you know one thing? The spirits behind the religions, I mean, the spirits in our midst, are spirits of ignorance, are very stubborn as little as they are, and are very powerful in times of tricks. So, if the spirits are by tricks, doing something against somebody and the person/people are not aware, they will have no choice but to continue what they are doing, even magnifying it differently. This is the type of mistake our ancestors made over religion in the hands of the familiar spirits. Because of that mistake, religion has been from Idol worship ringing on to modern-day religion. Could you imagine how many ages ago? and what does it take to avoid a reputation for mistakes? Little did I know, all it takes to avoid another mistake from the spirits monitoring every individual is nothing more than awareness. Once you are aware that the unusual things happening around you are caused by the unusual spirits monitoring you 24hrs. You keep meditating it day and night; you will see spirits now regard you as an enemy because you have understood their tricks. This means you are now very dangerous to them, which they will not like you disclosing to a third party.

Look at what is happening in today's families after a man and a woman have wedded together before the altar (white wedding, child dedication) or, before the idol shrines (traditional marriage, presentation of new-born babies) for they have now committed, in covenant/ agreement with these authorities: in these very passages, I will do my very best to make the meanings and the reasons very clear for us to understand. First off, we have discovered the authority of the entire religion and also have had a bit of understanding of what they can do and what they cannot do, which means their power is limited. So, without further delay, with these revelations, I will give us some reasons and points to open up our inner minds wider for awareness.

Look, sometimes, humans wonder over many things. Mostly, reasoning ways bible Creators are doing it. Without realizing that, most of these happen according to their nature, even in the past.

Here are some illustrations:

There is a man, a freethinker, and a lady, a partial Catholic; both sides of the divide were civil servants. As they met and were in love, in the course, both got married living together. To the extent, the love they have for each other did not give the lady and her entire family consent to remember taking the man to the Altar for wedlock, nor to the registry. Also, for the cause, the man is a freethinker; he did not even think about it. Both were happily married and living together. As time went by, after a couple of years of living together, the lady conceived and gave birth to a baby boy. The baby boy seemed like a coupon copy of the father, and for this, the man decided to set up a big party to name the child; all friends, families, and relatives were all invited.

To the greatest surprise, this family had five children, three boys and two girls aged 53 and 47. Before, they decided to stop concession, and by the time they were a bit older, their

Urgent Attention, Singles

first daughter got married to a fellow mate from the same university immediately after she graduated. Then, while sharing their experiences, the lady suggested following the footstep of her parents. She added that she believes that the single most crucial factor in a successful marriage is how they respond or react to the actions or attitudes of each other. So the newly married couple decided to take that step, and today, both were happily living together with their children.

You may ask, due to modern law, how, in any case, can a man and a woman live together and have children without wedlock or documentaries from the registry?

Accidentally, the problem came to the extent of separation in-between, and they brought the case to the court. How is the marriage going to be acknowledged by the court? Yes, it is quiet and straightforward; the court knows how to sort such issues out. Let's assume that a fight breaks up between two tribes or two people, and the police get involved, and this is similar to the point in question.

The point is that Governments have less interest in things of Religions. If not, the Governments want the number of divorced Marriages to diminish. The Governments supposed set outlaws, and in the course — any split in the union that will bring to the attention of the Court hearing. After the Court. The winner of the case will have 75%, while the quilting party will have a lesser procession of 25%. For assault/for breaking the law. For the fact that the world is civilizing day after day. If the Governments want divorce Marriage to stop increasing, let's stop making processions equal in divorce marriages.

If every Government sticks to this, you find out the split in Marriages will reduce because no one will admit to having lesser processions of his/her wealth. At the same time, help couples sort out/settle indoors whatever problem comes in between. That will also help a lot of people going into marriage these days to be extremely vigilant and careful who they choose. Split in the marital issue is the foundation of today's world problems. Started right from the bible, Adam, and Eve, which have been ring-ling on in families, affecting children and great-grandchildren. And in the Governments from generation to generation to this day. Why? Because of the very desperate spirits/influences behind the divorce, marriage is still in our midst.

It is quite understandable, logically that after the Creator, let assume, has created everything in the Garden according to the scriptures and handed it over to the Adam and Eve. And does not wholeheartedly depart from them, means, the beings are keeping eyes on this family, watching them, just because of all the things in possessions and also. Because of many other things, these authorities have in mind, in plans for humanity.

A further illustration is this. There is a man with a calling into ministerial works in his life. After he had gotten married to a lady, and after all, the traditional marriage was said and done, On the day of their white wedding, a considerable number of people from different places attended their wedding ceremonies. Unfortunately, this couple had a problem in conception; during the process, the couple set up a church; in the course, after Seven Years of the running of the church, the wife conceived and gave birth to a baby girl. Later on, the problem of concession started all over again. Twenty years later, the couple has many church branches all over the place under their ministries. Along the line, the family started having problems in their marriage. Then, after a bit of quiet with each other, the problem affects their ministries to the extent that the woman takes the case to court for a split. On the day of court negotiations, the court decided that they should stay apart from each other to avoid further conflict. Their processions/Ministries were divided into two parts, and also the court concluded that their only Daughter would accompany the Mother.

Within times after the separation, the Woman started running off her portion of the Ministries with their Daughter. After a couple of years, their daughter, at different intervals, received prophetic messages from the Elders in/of the Church that she had a calling into Ministry in Her Life. In the course, through prophecy, the Lady got married to one of the Ushers in the same Church. After their university studies, they started planning for the wedding. On the day of their Marriage, after the Wedding ceremonies, the Lady was also Anointed/Ordained as a Minister by the Mother, the Senior Minister of her Church, before all the invitees. After years of accompanying the Mother in the Ministry, the Lady set up Her Church at/in a different location with the newly Married Husband.

After a couple of Six Years in Her Ministry and in Her Marital life, the Lady is still without a Child. During this, circumstances made the Husband negotiate and secretly marry somebody else, which brought misunderstanding between the couple. To the extent that as time goes by, the Man later quietly has his way with the new Wife. Along the line, circumstances which the Ex-Wife could not be able to bear and at the same time running of the Church. The Lady decided to quietly close down her Church and went back to accompany the Mother in her Ministry. Now the Lady, the new Minister, and the Mother are single Pastoring Church and both looking for somebody else to get Married.

I do not know if you are following? I mean, people go through a lot in life without understanding the course, regardless of faith.

Now, a Mother (A Minister) and her Daughter (A Minister) single preaching the gospels, waiting and praying for their right partner. Two to Three years, nothing works out. It is quiet understandable that once a name becomes an active member/worker in a Church looking for a life partner, by the rules of the Church, the person cannot be Married in the same Church without the confirmation (Go ahead) of the authorities through the seniors/founders. Which means any marriage that will happen in a Church must be confirmed before that can be possible, mostly in these modern churches.

Again, we all are aware that the authorities can find a life partner among the congregation for any of these Ministers in less than one year. However, that's not done because the spirits want them to stay a bit longer, being single. Why? Mostly because by the time they are informed to the right person, there will be no excuse than to comply. The Church authorities are spirits of strategies in manipulation. As we know, no how these two Ministers will choose a life partner within the congregation without the consent/approval of the authorities/Spirits and likewise to another dedicated member.

However, here are the tricks of these authorities before the congregation in the issues of marriage. They are to give you something lower/cheaper than what you most need, in order not to keep away from praying for their help.

The authorities, by contradiction, their works are defined as steal, kill and destroy? An example is the story of Laban, Jacob, Leah, and Rachel in the bible. That's the reason a good percentage of singles are in every corner of the Church, waiting and praying to bring their life partner along their way without alternatives in their situations.

That mostly happened because of nature, the character of the beings in our midst, which have no regard for anybody; this is the secret I would like us to realize. For this, people go through a lot because of not having the recognition of the beings around every single person day and night, not to think of what they are capable of doing against us? If I say to you that every individual is like a newborn baby before these authorities in times of deception, I do not think I am mistaken.

The scripture says that the heart of a king (man) is in the hand of the Lord (spirits) like rivers of water. He (Spirit) turns it wherever He (Spirit) wishes.

Once more, if I say to you that what Jesus went through and what happened to Adam and Eve in the Garden are examples, an adage of what the beings had in mind for us individual lives. In our Marriages and not that they have been an existing Jesus that suffered Hell before and likewise the name Adam and Eve.

So, do you know that there was a time when the Ancestors used to present Newborn babies before the Shrines for protection? The Churches are also doing this today by way of Child dedication before the Altar for protection. The

Ancestors would take a newly born Baby with presents to the Shrines. They used a lot of Animal Blood, Palm Wine, and cola nuts for sacrifice, and they were doing all these without knowing that they were worshipping the familiar Spirits — that's a firm Covenant unaware.

Again, I say to you that both to present new-born Babies before the Shrines for protection, Child dedication before the Altar for protection, traditional Marriage, and white Weddings are all likened to the Covenant of Adam and Eve in the Garden. With the Spirits, which means under the authority of the same Spirits, called Ancestral Spirits? They exist as Male and Female, reproducing through the laying of eggs in the green glass, which is the Satan/devils.

So they are no strangers here on Earth; they are also indigent of the world; they are the world authorities and also authorities of the entire religion. That's where our entire problem reclines. This is also why strange happening even in the house of the Ministers of the Gospels. That is the main reason the scriptures, by illustration/proverb, tell us about the suffering of Jesus. (Ministers of the worlds)

Further Illustrations:

As these authorities calmed, he then created Eve from the rib of the Adam, brought her to Adam, and he (Adam) received her. To be a companion to him, which means marriage? The spirit has now joined and wedded them together. This means Adam, said yes, I do, and received her, which means this family is now in agreement? In covenant with these authorities, like vast numbers of men, have said yes, I do. Now and then, and received their companions before alter. Before the wedding assembles, therefore, the conflict/split of Adam and Eve in the Garden (Entire World) is caused by the serpent (Spirits).

Both illustrations are an adage. Proverbs of what beings have in stocks, in plans for the people of this age in times of marriage. I do not know if this is very clear? That's why marriage splits also take place in the House of the Ministers of the Gospels.

For these reasons, that is also where these authorities contradicted its meaning; these are the ways these authorities operate in our families. It is quite understandable that the same beings that have joined Adam and Eve (a couple) together are also equal beings, which, by the nature of ruse, brought misunderstanding between the same couple. That resulted in the division. So, that's what is happening in the families today. That is after a man and a woman have joined or welded together before the idol shrines (traditional marriage, presentation of new-born babies) or before the altar (white wedding or child dedication). For these, these people/families have now committed, in the covenant, in agreement with these authorities. As this revelation explained and exposed, the works of these authorities are defined as steal, kill, and destroy. Please, let's not ignore the fact, in reality, that's why we have a vast number of families that have been torn apart in the world today without a solution. Even in the house of the ministers of the gospels because they do not respect anybody. Due to their evil nature. As a result, if I say to you, every marital home is regarded as the foundation of the Entire World before these authorities. That is another reason why the beings used Adam and Eve as the foundation, the First Man and the First Woman in the bible. Therefore, the stories of Adam and his wife, Eve, are the way they operate in marital homes and not that both are the First Man and the First Woman that existed before. No, sir. No, ma.

Urgent Attention, Singles

A further explanation: After they have claimed to have created Adam and Eve, they joined (wedded) them together and handed them all the things in the Garden (Entire World) and at the same time banned them from the forbidden tree amid the Garden. Also, as the serpent deceived the couple through the woman and the couple tampered with the forbidding tree, which the authorities know quite well, that will surely take place because they stimulate the woman.

Now, for these, cures came upon them, and from there, misunderstanding and split started. First place, the Generational Curse was established upon all the living by the Spirits.

Means an adage, a proverb to the Entire World, through the bible, first man and the first woman. Consequently, it merely says that any man and woman joined/wedded as husband and wife is now like Adam and Eve. Regardless of the faith. That has also tampered with that forbidden tree, and at the same time, the curse that was placed upon Adam and Eve is also upon them. That has now broken because it has been exposed. Their tricks have been presented before us, but mind you, their chances depend on the couples concerned. As a fact, that makes misunderstandings and splits also happen, even in the families of the

Ministers through unforeseen influences. If not, it should not have to the representative's Ministers.

Now, with these revelations, it is quite understandable that once two have joined together, they are now under these authority's laws; as it says, those who know the rules are mostly bound under the law—that is why you mostly find misunderstanding and splits in today's marital homes. I mean, with modern people, more than with the people in those days. The ancestors because the same desperate beings are still in our midst.

With these experiences, I have discovered that where there is wealth, it is mostly where to found splits in marriages. Or maybe in a family, where the women are more opportune in income than the man, I mean, more educated, which allowed her to earn higher wages than the husband. However, do not forget that it happens on both sides. This is the most common reason we can find divorces in marriages uncontrolled in the Western world, then in third-world countries. These authorities capitalize on the possessions/wealth of couples. Likewise, in what

Urgent Attention, Singles

people are doing to bring misunderstanding in their midst, their chances depend on the couples concerned.

The family of Adam was attacked by the serpent through the influences of Eve. Due to the possessions under them in the Garden. Therefore, which means? Before, attacks will come to any family to the point of misunderstanding and will lead to split; there must be something the spirits will capitalize on to cause envy and jealousy, which will lead to divisions. Therefore, what every couple should be aware of is this. Once you have come together as a family, like Adam and Eve, always have in mind. There are pretty sure (a must) numbers of these spirits that walk and monitor your day and night. Because you agree, in covenant with them, on like Adam and Eve.

As these revelations explained and exposed, the works of these beings are defined as steal, kill, and destroy. If I said that Jesus's story and everything about him at the Cross and in his Ministerial works is also an adage. A proverb of what they had in plans for the representative ministers here on Earth. I do not think I'm kidding. This will also help us comprehend that there has never been a Jesus that existed before. Then, what they are trying to let the representative's ministers understand is that they do not respect a name, even of his son, let alone the representatives here on Earth in times of their authority. Also, their requirements in their business.

With these revelations, the real meaning of Jesus is a well-known Minister, and the 12 disciples of Jesus are the elders in his Ministries. Therefore, what the scriptures say Jesus went through. Is an example of what some of today's Ministers? It is also a kind of encouragement to what may rise to any of the representative ministers here on Earth. So, not that there has been an existing Jesus that went through hell before. It also allows us to realize that a vast number of people, mostly the faiths, have wasted years. We are fooling ourselves in the hands of the natural spirit beings.

NO WED, STILL

Again, the characters and the plans of the beings, towards a name trying to settle down. Regardless of the faith, it is made clear in the stories of Jacob, Laban, Leah, and Rachel (Genesis29;15). It says, "Then Laban said to Jacob, because you are my relatives, should you, therefore, serve me for nothing? Tell me, what should your wages be?" "Now Laban had two daughters, the name of the elder was Leah, and the name of the younger one was Rachael." It also says that "Leah's eyes were delicate, but Rachael was beautiful of form and appearance and (V: 18) says, "Now Jacob loved Rachael."

So he said, "I will serve you seven years for Rachael, your younger daughter. Laban said," It is better that I give her to you than that I should give her to another man." So

Jacob served seven years for Rachel, and they seemed only a few days to him because of the love he had for her." Then Jacob said to Laban, give me my wife for my days fulfilled, that I may go into her." "And Laban gathered together all the men of the place and feast. "Now it came to pass in the evening, he took Leah, his daughter, and brought her to Jacob, and he went in with her." And Laban gave his maid Zilpah to his daughter Leah as a maid. "So it came to pass in the morning that beholds, it was Leah, and he said to Laban, what is this, you have done unto me? Was it not for Rachel I served you? Why, then have you deceived me?

I do not know if you understand the story correctly? Well, I suppose you did.

Lastly, in reality, that's the way the beings operate amid the congregation. In our families, in societies, and in the World at large. These are the reasons families and the World as a whole is full of divisions, misunderstandings, problems, and hardships all over the place. We can also witness how Laban is used by the beings to set confusion amid these three brethren as to the way people have been used by unforeseen influences to deny huge numbers their rights in marriages, in the place of work, and mostly in the Government offices. The desperate humans' opposition

No Wed, Still

found it very difficult to do things without the use the motivation of people who know you or around you without those humans realizing the influences behind their doing. Yet, their success only depends on the name concerned. So, my dear reader, the scriptures above is typically a kind of signal or, a reflection of the characteristics.

However, this is precisely the way they operate. Every one of their actions is guided by jealousy. You can witness that after Laban had made an agreement with Jacob for the contract of Rachel. When Jacob fulfills that contract because of jealousy, the beings subsist by making Laban give Jacob Leah instead of Rachel. Again, these authorities have a very high degree in substitute confusion. Laban wanted to confuse Jacob by inviting all their relatives for the marriage feast of Jacob and Rachel. Despite all, Laban still went on to fulfil his intentions to Jacob by giving him Leah in midnight instead of Rachel. Because of the jealousy of giving out his beautiful daughter to Jacob, he decided to provide him with Leah.

I do not know if you understand this story properly? Firstly, Jacob did not tell Laban that he wanted to marry two wives. However, he ended up with two wives and their housemaids. As to reflection of the character of the authorities of the entire religion, if the beings could not find any other thing to do to us, to get us down, they will begin to bring us all kinds of substitutes for what a person may have needed. Whether you like it or not, they will be doing all these for some reason. First is out of jealousy. Second is that beings do not initially want you to achieve Success. So, as to the purpose, Jacob was provided with a surplus to weigh him down. Do not forget that Jacob was a man whose families had a covenant with these authorities right from Abraham and is like Laban, who was an unbeliever.

As to the way they operate before congregates. A single sister or a brother may be dreaming and assuming somebody in the church for a life partner, and the authorities know everyone in there—their family background, including their educational level. Also, know who to link you up with, and things will be alright for the couple. Still, they are not ready to do that. Instead, they will bring you somebody that both of you will keep on struggling in life. Please do not misunderstand me. I have not said that these authorities cannot give you a right life partner or exactly your choice of partner. No, they can do that. Still, one out of a hundred, so that both of you will keep on surviving in order not to be absent in the Church services or backslide.

The story above is also supposed to give us the background information of the bible's words. Based on the human's ideas of life and leadership, imitated by the beings and con us to believe. So do not you ever neglect the tricks of them or take them for granted in times of deception. Well, it's great that Jacob is a man who knows what he wants and does not allow manipulation to get him down. For this, he insisted and got what he wanted at first. So, now, for better achievement, I suppose, in our individual lives, this should be an excellent lesson for all of us.

Have caused the Entire World, damages, disappointments and setbacks, due to mistake and early life of the Ancestors. The Earth is the paradise for all the living, final stopping:

To witness to us that these beings have limited power also disqualifies them completely. In understanding and experiences, I would first do my very best to share some of the things they are capable of doing, as I have mentioned somewhere that the leading beings are capable of bringing anything to do with conviction. If not, forget about it. Now, I will give you some examples of what the conviction of the beings can do in the life of the living.

Firstly, they are capable of making someone frequently lose memory and never recall those things anymore. Because the very beings doing it are always with them, day and night, without giving the person an inch distance or gap. That's one of their tricks against students, mostly during exams businessmen and women and those in authorities.

Likewise, on the other hand, they can make someone to remember something or keep thinking and meditating over an issue, mostly when someone is disfavoured. These living beings are capable of doing this because they can reason what a person has in their inner mind. That explains the main reason humans are easily deceived by their rights from their ancestors.

Now, pay attention to this story. One of the examples of what conviction can do in people's lives is this. In one of the Churches I attended, it happened after the church came into the very building, which was a two-story building. However, as of that time, they rented the first floor for their use. The family that owns the building was making use of another part of the building. Again, by the time the church was celebrating one of her anniversaries, after the real feasts, they started growing and multiplying greatly. Then, after a couple of months, the owner of the building began complaining to the senior minister about the noise coming from the church music. However, because of this, the church was doing its best to minimize disturbances. Could you believe it? By the time the church was getting to one year at the building and doing all their best to minimize disruptions as they could? However, the landlord continued to complain to the point of going to the council, and in the process, the court was involved.

The Ministers did not keep quiet over the issue. They did their best by praying for intervention. Then, it happened that as they were praying about it, the Landlord still maintained that the Church must move out. At a point, it seemed everything was getting out of hand. However, it happens that one night, a vision was given to the Senior Minister. In this vision, he saw himself tying the Landlord and his Family with rope and carrying them out in front of the very Church Building. This means the process of making the man and his family be Church tenants in the very same building the Church has been renting from him for some time?

Then, during this case, the Landlord had already taken the matter to Court. However, surprisingly, before the day of the hearing, the Landlord called the Pastor to ask him if the Church would like to buy the property. He was telling them to depart. However, the Pastor said to him that he would get back to him. After that, the Minister went to pray about the proposal. Nonetheless, before the day of the Court hearing, the Pastor concluded/agreed with the Landlord for the purchase of the property.

Next, the Landlord went and withdrew the case from the Court and had to pay the first month's rent to the Church. So that is how the Landlord turned out to be the tenant of the Church as foretold in a vision. These also are what are called the conviction's power of the Spirits in their operation against the living.

Now, in this case, you will be able to realise that the landlord was really out of mind all this while. It all happened within 18 months from the time the Church moved into the building and the time the Church bought the property from the landlord.

Can you imagine, after complaints from the landlord, and within the time, he issued a case to the Council and even went to the Court? Still, later, the Man withdraws from the situation and decides to sell the property to the Church. Signifies the working power/convictions of these authorities.

Mind you, people, due encounter a similar situation in different ways regardless of their faith.

Then, two years later, in the same Church and still under the same conviction, a prophecy was given to the Minister. The prophecy was that all the Workers and anyone among the congregation willing to join to contribute one thousand pounds each to enable the Church to pay off the mortgage arenas of the very Church Building. The two-storey paid off under two years of purchase is backed up with bible reference (Numbers 1; 1-2).

After the contribution, the Church Mortgage paid off, so you can witness that the conviction of these authorities is compelling. So far, the beings are concerned in times of tricks. That is what the authorities use by emptying the pocket of the faiths. They do not struggle over this, very quietly in what they can do.

That's similar to what I narrated before, which happened in my place of work. Where a private business of my boss was shown to me in a Night vision. Egyptians were negotiating with my boss to buy the company, which was later sold to them just for me to lose my job during the course/trials of which the beings discovered to be otherwise. After the deal was done, I lost the job. My boss is not aware of the influences behind what he did. Still, I do, because of spiritual understanding. So when such a situation occurs, the name involved will never, ever know what is happening to him until the plans of the beings are over.

It is to tell us that the conviction of these authorities is compelling mostly to novices, and such happens to high numbers of us, private businesses' and companies' owners unaware, regardless of faith.

Further examples of the conviction that happened at the end of 1997: At that time, I became a real Christian. One day, I was so excited that I decided to buy a musical set and some home furniture to settle down.

On that day, I decided to go to one of the electronics shops on Tottenham Court Road in Central London. I had on me about 1,270 GBP to go for one of the best electronics, a five-piece audio system, which cost about 1.230 GBP as of December 1997. However, instead of buying these home entertainment sets as planned, I decided to while away time because I was contemplating whether or not to buy the musical.

After considering it for two hours, I decided to go home without buying anything. Then, as I got back that day without buying any, I was furious in my spirit, regretting why I could not buy any.

Nevertheless, I decided to go back next Saturday to buy this product. However, it happened that as I was about 5 minutes away from the shop the second time, the same thought came back again, and I started contemplating the second time. Even so, I still decided to go home without buying anything a second time.

Then, after about 2 or 3 weeks in January of the next year, the spirit (Church authorities) told me to thank Him with something as a result of the vow I made one time ago during prayer. That made me buy a Van and give it to the Church for Thanksgiving. I hope you can see how spirits operate if I had purchased these musical sets that time as intended. It could not have been possible for me to have bought the Van for my Church, so all this time, I was battling with my mind over buying the musical sets, the spirits. That is monitoring me all along is behind it. However, I did not know what was behind it then. Therefore, when it comes to convicting people from their initial plans, the beings are perfect on how they use to shift people. Mostly, single and couples do what is supposed to be right for them.

Did you know the hardest thing that can happen to the spirit (devil) in charge of a name is to be killed? Let me give you a reference so that you get my point. For example, Russians and Ukraine were fighting today. By accident (Satan), Putin or Zelenskyy, the leader of the War, was killed. Could you imagine what it will look like? That is exactly what it means to kill a Satan in charge of a name, which is what spirits hate to hear. So, these are the main reasons the lady was not allowed to get closer to me because I said I would kill those spirits that had been attacking her all along, which also made them stir the lady to call the police for me to block me from having further communication with her so that they will not be killed.

No Wed, Still

Because if we eventually get together, I will do my best to kill those spirits, which they know is likely.

Did you know why the lady started parking her car just opposite my window after she called the police? She did that pretending to still be with me, which will move me to call or text her again; that's another dangerous trap for me, which will result in a second coming of the police against me and which may trigger the police to relocate my living somewhere else. The devils don't' want the lady to see me with her eyes anymore because seeing me will help her think of me, which the spirits don't want. Suppose the lady was not newly relocated to that very building by the Council. In that case, the easiest thing the spirits should have done is to stir the lady to park out from that building to somewhere else in order not to see me anymore. But that is not possible. Then, by ticks, they are now negotiating another possible way to separate the two of us from that very building. But the lady without spiritual understanding does not understand what was behind her all along.

Well, for the reasons she arranged police for me, I stopped going through her passage to my apartment from that day. When she took notice, she insisted on parting opposites my window. I later grasped through her body language that she started parking her car opposite my window after the police because she didn't want us to become enemies; she wanted us to remain friends. To help her move freely in the estate, but if we become enemies, she will feel too shy moving around witting the estate because she is a shy lady. So, dear, give it a reason?

Little did I know, if you are a man or a woman and due to religious doctrines, you are covering your hair with a headscarf, Rev, Sisters, etc., better stop doing that, for the devil is a liar. Okay, now you have witnessed all the tricks of these spirits, the authorities of the entire world's religion. I mean, whatever doctrine in any religion today must be suggested by the spirits or the authorities of religion. As we know, the devil is a liar, and their works are defined as stealing, killing, and destroying. The three things that define their works are that nothing good comes from them, so they are not profitable to humanity. Now, to expose you to tricks, did you know that the devils are so jealous of men and women, especially our women? I hope you have heard about spiritual husbands and how it works. If not, please do yourself a favour and go through my books and find out where I talked about the Spirits that are familiar to man; whatever men enjoy, so are the spirits; therefore, women are also good to the spirits. These are the main reasons for religious doctrines. Women are suggested to be covering their hair so that men will not take notice, for hair is a woman's beauty.

Shyness, why? But the reason is that many men and women, regardless of colour, mostly women, feel shy even within their families. Please pay attention here. I am here to deliver you from shyness. If you believe, please do what I ask you to do? Shyness is of the devil. As described earlier in these books the number of spirits that monitors every individual in the World.

SPIRIT'S CONVICTION

Hence, those spirits monitoring you 24 hours a day are the cause of your shyness. Maybe in your family or elsewhere. And they are completely nothing to human beings, and they can stop that once they take notice that now you understand tricks. Still, if you do not care about what they are doing, then they will continue doing it because they are spirits of ignorance, very stubbornness, and brutality, as little as they are.

Let me give an example of what shyness is all about and what it does. I can remember one of my late sisters. I mean, this lady was full of shyness all over her, and not that she wasn't tall and beautiful enough. To the point she found it difficult to go over amid a crowd. Instead, she would like to go over a crowd with her face down by slipping through the side of the crowd. If it happens she accidentally encounters one of her relatives who is not relating well with her, she will shrink under the ground before that person, and if you want to finish her, just seriously tell her that you hate her; I mean, never will she like come near you as long as she lives, due to shyness. Occasionally, you will see some people at every moment they make unnecessary phone calls when they feel shy before people or use eyeglasses to cover their faces.

Suppose I say that shyness is transferable because it is caused by those familiar spirits who monitor everyone. In that case, I don't think I have gone wrong. In a family, let's assume your Mom is a shy lady; you find out that her daughters may become shy too because those spirits that make the Mom shy are 24 hours there without option. These are reasons you will find out that some people find it difficult to stand alone and defend themselves in a serious situation. Without somebody standing along with them, these mostly happened to ladies, no matter the qualifications.

Due to the transferability of these, you found out that some countries' lifestyles have become part of it, that anytime somebody from such a country will be having issues with an outsider, the person will invite a third party to stand alongside him/her. I am not sure if you are getting my points. Not even to invite a third party once those people see their people talking with outsiders, immediately the person will meet them up and stand with the relatives. It has become part of them and continues that way from generation to generation, which means generational. Course. Because the spirits behind it are record keepers, they are ready to keep a record of things for years. Stubborn spirits that are worth nothing to humans, just only because by their tricks, humans were taken unaware.

So, my dear, not being bold enough is of familiar spirits that know you right from your baby age, and those spirits can be found in the hairs of your head, within the clothes you wear, at the back of your neck, and even sometimes can be found in your face, the most wicked ones. If you want it to stop, start meditating on that day and night, and let them know that now you understand their tricks. If you don't mind and want to kill them, just put gum in your hand; anytime you feel such, apply gum within the place I mentioned; if they see your seriousness about it, they will keep off because they hate to be killed and will not like you to disclose tricks to the third party.

As human nature, children who are not properly brought up well by parent's guardians greatly affect their lifespan. These are reasons some people's behaviour is seen as incomplete. Let's assume that a man gets married to a lady and they have given birth to four, 2 boys and 2 girls; on the way to bringing the children, unintentionally, they break-up, and the Court decides the children will accompany the lady. Now, the children were living with their Mum and missing their father's hood. So, the children will know how to experience their father's guardians and likewise the other side of it. That father's spirit is missing inside those children, irrespective of age. Those children have only their mother's spirit inside them.

Another example of the point is, if you are a good observer, you will be able to notice this in a family where parents have produced 4 or 5 females without a male child; you can see that those 5 girls will be missing a male child within them and these have resulted at that their young age any man that approaches any of them for whatever that is it. Sometimes, the children will ask their Mum to give them a male child, which will stir those girls up to keep the focus on me because no one fathered them, even until their adult age. Remember, it happened likewise on the other side of it. This has resulted mostly in the advanced countries where break ups are widespread, to be seen girls between the ages 13, 14,15, to 16 years of age, sometimes seen some girls of the above age with their own kids, young single Mothers, and single Fathers. I mean, go to some Cities in the US or in London, like Brixton and Lewisham, all in London, and witness the very common points. And when any of them find themselves in that kind of situation, they find it difficult to further their career, which will automatically help them find themselves in social assistance.

Spirits in our midst are very brutal, in times of tricks, helping spouses break up in order for their children not to be brought up properly with good manners; these tricks are one of the 3 titles that define the works of the spirits: destruction. As we know, as spirits monitor, those young single mothers and single fathers surely will be helping them to continue living the way their parents lived, and it continues that way. I suggest, if this is possible, in a breakup family, even If the Court decides that the children will be with the lady, it is better for at least 2 times a week

Spirit's Conviction

to allow the children intervals paying visits to their father whilst living with their Mum, especially during vacation, I think that will aid the children experiencing father's hood in their lifespan.

Spirits of disagreement produce spirits of separation; remember what happened between Adam and their Wife, Eve, in the Garden of Eden. Please, if you know that intervals, you disagree with your spouse, boss, manager at work, or uncle. Or even your parents etc., That means you need to be watchful. Mind you, not that there will not be disagreements in between, but not in every issue, but if it happened to be rampant, it would be very dangerous. Because it is only through disagreeing with one another that the spirits stand to attack both of you. So, if you know what will bring disagreement in-between, try to avoid it. The devil is always there, reluctantly triggering the issue, particularly now they are unhappy because of exposing tricks.

But where do you think these spirits of separation can be found? If you have been through these 2 books, Greatest Mistake and Sharp Minded Criminals, you must have known that, but if you don't? Be careful here; if you meditate over an issue now, God, that means Spirits hear it immediately. Therefore, those spirits that hear you are not different from the spirits that cause separation between the spouse and can be found within the clothes you wear and within the hairs of your head; the Bible says that your body is the temple of the holy ghost and inside your house attentively listening to whatever is going on in your house, could you imagine, very dangerous.

Likewise, in a polygamous family, where two or more women are married to one man, never will spirits allow those women to stand to see each other regardless of faith. Maybe one out of a hundred will stand and see each other. The same occurred to the first male child of each of the women; spirits will never allow that first male to frequently communicate with each other as a family member, likewise on their first daughters, just to create divisions in these families.

Now, the solution to these above, first and foremost, is that when things are happening around us, we do our best to discover the cause, the roots, and how to solve the concern. Meanwhile, cast the mind back to the Garden of Eden, Adam and Eve lived together in peace until the serpent came in between; that's when they started having problems that triggered them to be disobedient.

Therefore, human beings cherish each other (*Genesis*11:4). Then they said, "Come, let us build ourselves a city, with a tower that reaches to the heavens, so that we may make a name for ourselves. But because of the Spirits World in our midst, that cherished has now become envy towards our fellow human beings. An example can be found in (*Genesis*11:7) Says, come let Us go down and confuse their language so that they will not understand one another's speech." Hope you understand what it means? Do you want the misunderstanding in your family to end? Up? From the day you made that decision, then you need to be angry with those familiar spirits monitoring you and, likewise, everyone; speak it out to their hearing that now you have understood their tricks, and tell them to keep off from your family. If not, you will find ways to kill them; quote me, and they will be cautious.

Now, let's talk about spirits of annoyance and anger. If you know that sometimes anger has become part of your life, and you have done your best to get it under control, and it is seen as impossible? Then, you need to deliver yourself from that slavery. Anger and shyness are likening together and are slavery. Do you know how devil tricks work out for them? Let me give you an example of how it worked. As have explained in one of my books, Greatest Mistake, how familiar spirits first give an ancestor a tale story of a King that lives in the sky. This happened after the given story. The ancestor did not reason it and believed everything the spirits said to him. Then, spirits have no choice but to keep magnifying the tale of a king who lives in the sky because one man believed together with his family, and it continues that way up to today. That's why even modern people have joined in magnifying and evangelising about a great King that lives in the sky (Heaven).

So dearly beloved, that's how it occurs to somebody that any little thing the person will get angry because the person has initially unknowingly accepted and entertained that anger. Look, let me tell you I am qualified to educate you about the spirits in our midst because, for over 20 years, we have been fighting and killing them. I am not kidding you. Therefore, the spirits that sometimes stir you to get angry with someone are those spirits that monitor you 24hrs. They have been doing that because, at first, they tried it on you, you accepted it, and because of their stubbornness, they have no option but to continue it on you. Let's assume that at first, they tried it on you, you ignored it by not being angry, and if they tried it on you a couple of times, you rejected it. Quote me, they will keep off doing it. They may have assumed now you understand that's the devil because they won't like you if you reason it that way. But if, at first, they stir you and you respond by being angry, then the spirit will have no choice but to continue doing it against you; any slight disagreement you had with somebody immediately spirits will rest on you to course spirits of anger.

Pregnant women: Let me expose you more to the spirit's tricks; here are the tricks spirits use right from origin to spread spirits of anger to all humans. Just to witness the height of wickedness of the spirits behind the religion. Hope you are aware that whatever is happening to a pregnant woman negatively or positively also affects the baby in the womb. Okay, now listen to this. Have you asked yourself why pregnant women get angry more quickly than others? Or I don't know if you have noticed how pregnant women get angry. The annoyance of a pregnant woman is caused by those spirits monitoring her 24 hours a day for ages. We are intentionally doing that for many reasons. First, the spirits stir the pregnant woman, which causes her to be angry in every little thing you see on her framing face. Secondly, the spirits purposely did that to affect the child in the womb. That means if spirits of anger remain with the child throughout a lifetime, every little thing with somebody he/she will become angry quickly, and it continues that way.

Okay, now how do spirits get pregnant women or somebody angry about a little issue? As they monitor you, they already know what upsets you and what doesn't. So anytime you're having issues with someone, once those spirits rest on your head and face and breathe into your nose and the person breath it in, the person's face will Change, look ugly, and from there, become angry at once and suppose you carefully look at the woman's face at that moment. In that case, it will somehow look ugly, like a bad woman (bad boy). And as we know, as the lady is breathing that polluted air, the child in the womb is breathing it too. And if the lady becomes angry, the child in the womb is also affected.

These are the main reasons why after a woman has given birth to a baby, any little thing, the baby will start crying and panicking, just because of that pollutes air from the spirit that enters the child through the mum, and it continues that way. So please, pregnant women, do your best to get yourself under control, mostly when having issues with somebody once the devils are there to mess your mind up and will affect the child in the womb.

Uncertain, you know sometimes sleep comes to your eye unexpectedly even when you are busy doing something, maybe whilst driving, studying, cooking or something else.80% of people falling asleep unexpectedly are, of course, by those spirits monitoring them day and night. Those spirits doing that can be found in your eyelids as little as they are, within your chest, stepping within the clothes you are wearing, and at the back of your neck within the Collar of your clothes.

Cut those hairs down? Please help me advise that guy and your friend to cut those hairs. I noticed one terrible thing, and I will take my time to make it known to those who care. As have details in one of the books on how spirits lay eggs and have their issues in the green glasses. Therefore, so sorry to hear that spirits in our minds regard human hair as green grasses, which are reasons mostly found in human hair more than any other body parts. Scripture says your body is the temple of the Holy Ghost. (1*Corinthians* 6:19) this is a proverb of the Spirits to you and me. Have given examples of the numbers of spirits monitoring every individual in one of the books. Today, all the tricks of the Spirits in our midst have been exposed.

Before I continue on the topic above, let's talk about this: too many of us do not know the difference between Satan and the Devil. I will take my time to clarify it in a way you will understand. Before, when I was not into religion, I used to assume or expect Satan or devils somehow in a human form. But when I became a Christian, that was when I realised how they looked and appeared. Some people, even if they are not religious, maybe see Spirits called Satan or devils without identifying that this is it because they are 24 hours with you monitoring all you are doing without option, and the easiest place to notice them is in your hair.

Satan and the devils have not gotten much different but in different categories or hierarchies. Among the numbers of spirits monitoring an individual, the one called Satan is the main spirit in charge of that person and also the one that first occupied that person immediately after the person was born, and the one that understands your inner thoughts and whatever message them have for you that the one to make it known to you and among all of them Satan is the most brutal. There may be too many monitoring you, but not all will understand your inner thoughts; only those who were also born and raised where the person was born and raised. When they have issues with the person they are monitoring, Satan may invite other wicked spirits who don't know the person to come and help them. Satan's decision is final on the person concerned.

Whilst other ones with Satan are called the devils. Devils not born where you were born and raised cannot understand your inner thoughts unless you meditate on the languages they understand.

Let's say you are fighting them, I mean, against those spirits, and you may be capable of killing them, but only the one called Satan you cannot be able to kill, not that is physically fit more than other spirits but very brutal, exceedingly wicked. And very vigilant at every given minute, any slightest thing he will fly, is full of fears and difficult to see Satan rest on the body of whom is in charge, rather keeps soaring within the person's shadow. Sharp-minded Criminal. Somebody may die today, and the Satan in charge of him may go into the coffin and bury the person with Satan to witness how wicked and hopeless the spirits are. All these are why it is very difficult to get him to kill. Similar to what is happening in the human military, liken to the Ukraine and Russian war, you may have killed all the Ultraism or Russian armies, but it is very difficult to get Putin or Zelenskyy killed; that is exactly with the Spirits in our midst, familiar spirits operate after manners of men.

Too many of us today are into poverty, one problem or the other without a solution. Sometimes, it may be because of what our forefathers did, or because of what we course (Additions) ourselves, or because of ignorance. The wicked spirits monitoring everyone capitalised on that and got their wicked job done. Let's assume today that 4 or 5 policemen are walking and monitoring somebody from morning till late; wherever the person goes, they are following him up and down. I think even if those officers didn't inform the person of their intention, as a human, you must discern that there is a danger, which allowed those officers to keep their focus on the person. This is similar to what I want you to reason with me regarding the intentions of Satan and devils in number monitoring every individual. Of which a huge number of us were unaware. These are major causes of the foundation of poverty in many families today. If police monitor you

Spirit's Conviction

today, you will be watchful of what you do. Therefore, I want you as a person to be exceedingly vigilant of Satan monitoring you even whilst asleep because Spirits do not sleep as we do; day and night, they are awake.

Now, let me go straight to the points, for example-- the story of the children of Israel, as the spirits have brought them out from their house of bondage (Egypt). While on their way to the promised land, they were all killed by the same spirits. -the scripture made us understand that after the children of Israel had left Egypt, some of them remained in the house of bondage (Idol worshipping). So likewise, today, modern religions head to Heaven as pronounced by the king (God the Spirit). Still, some modern people are there living in bondage through idolatry; these are the reasons the spirits take revenge.

Little did I know if we really understood the meaning of the words above. That still some of the modern people remained there, living in bondage through worshipping the idol and, for this, the spirit's revenge. Please, if you have ever imagined how wicked the spirits are, you will be able to know that Satan is not kidding. Could you imagine, right from the history of man, that they have been deceiving us until now? They mean what they have said. When we say, they are still living in bondage through worshipping the Idol. Now, I want us to understand this: living in bondage does not only when somebody goes to the shrine idol; one can still be living in bondage through other ways of traditional life, and let it be known to us other traditional ways of life, that typically means living in bondage. So far, these spirits are concerned, and they do not compromise over it. Another thing I would like us to comprehend is that spirits in the World are the same, and they operate in the same manner. Do not forget that now, as their tricks were discovered, Satan and the devils are now exceedingly wicked than ever before. against humans.

READERS WHERE HAVE YOU AFFECTED

Today, if I say to you that one of the things Spirits hate is seeing somebody being proud, bragging, or raising their shoulder (showing off), spirits hate it. Why? Because they regard human beings as nothing. As mentioned before, spirits regard human hairs like green glasses where spirits lay eggs and have their issues. Do you know that today, many families are seriously living in bondage unknowingly?

After my experiences in the wilderness of the spiritual world, or rather, the Church authorities, I have come to appreciate the companies that first introduced dating sites and blind dating. Just imagine how challenging it would be with the increasing number of single men and women in the world today. These tools have been instrumental in their efforts to reduce singleness, and it is often said that you don't realize the value of something until you lose it. Let me make this clear: witnessing the hate and animosity from the spiritual forces behind religion toward those who find quick and modern ways of getting married, such as open marriage systems even inside universities, devils are liars, and those who choose not to seek a spouse within the Church, is truly astonishing.

Here, I present the thoughts of the spirits behind the entire world's religions concerning single women, as revealed in the scripture (*Isaiah* 4:1): "On that day, seven women will take hold of one man and say, 'We will eat our own food and provide our own clothes; only let us be called by your name to take away our disgrace!'" This passage is reiterated, indicating that at a future time, seven women will seek one man to avoid the shame of being unmarried by providing for themselves but adopting him as their husband. Again, the proverbs remind us that it's not what goes into a man that defines him but what comes out of him.

Dear reader, if we haven't recognized it yet, the above scripture reflects the mindset of all the authorities in the world's religions. Now, let's consider the situation of single individuals in today's churches. Personally, I spent a total of six years in a local church, obediently waiting for God to confirm my life partner, not with any intention of becoming a minister. It may sound incredulous to some, but there were other brethren with the same purpose who stayed even longer. The rules in modern churches are truly astonishing.

As someone who has fought and experienced the wickedness of the evil spirits in our midst, I believe it's crucial for us to be open and discuss modern open marriages. These spirits are desperately wicked, especially now that their tricks have been exposed over a decade ago. Now, if I say to you that whosoever first introduced open marriage sites based solely on physical attraction, the evil spirits are behind it. The devil employs many tactics and stimulates spirits to set people up in different ways. Those with a good spiritual understanding can undoubtedly discern this.

The devil is cunning, and if his initial plans fail, he will find alternative ways to achieve his goals. This is how they operate: evil spirits, always opposing humanity. Therefore, those without spiritual understanding will not be able to see through their tricks. The scripture also states that the devil recognizes those who belong to him. So, when we see men and women seemingly joyous and enthusiastic on open marriage sites, we should question whether this is truly right. The devil's deception is real, and we should never underestimate the power of the spiritual world and what it can do. In marriage, your originality, I mean, where you come from and your bloodline matters most because it is for life. Even though the spirit is brutal; still they know what is best for you or me, and this is the lesson to learn from Isaac (Genesis 24) How was Isaac's wife chosen? Abraham sends his servant to his relatives in Mesopotamia to find a wife for his son Isaac. Yahweh provides the servant with a sign by sending Rebekah to give him and his ten camels water to drink. Rebekah is brought from her family to Isaac, who finds comfort in her after the death of his mother, Sarah. However, here are some common rules that many people in open marriages swear by:

- » Don't opt in for the wrong reasons.
- » Prioritize your marriage.
- » Don't let jealousy build.
- » Discuss safe sex.

- » Maintain open communication.
- » Agree on how you will explain your situation to outsiders.
- » Set sexual boundaries.
- » Set emotional boundaries.

Let's acknowledge this fact: when tempted by the devil, all the vows that spirits have been monitoring may be stolen from you, and you won't even remember them until the devil's intentions are fulfilled, depending on the circumstances. I hope you can bear witness to this. Among all the attendees of these open marriage sites in the Western world, it's rare to find guys over 30 years of age. Mostly, you'll encounter individuals between 20 to 26 years old. Can you imagine? Many are rushing into marriage without enough life experiences, and some have only just completed their college education, leaving behind their career aspirations as the devils push them reluctantly into marriage without their knowledge.

Let me clarify that I'm not saying finding a good life partner through open marriage sites is impossible. However, you need to be extremely vigilant in choosing the right person because the spirits are watching your marriage, just as they did with Adam and Eve in the Bible, seeking ways to affect your marriage. This becomes especially critical when your parents do not support your intentions. Recall what happened to Adam and Eve in the Garden, where the serpent (or spirit) influenced Eve, leading to their downfall.

On the other hand, is this the best approach to entering into marriage, or is it merely chosen for its speed? Not every family may be open to the idea of their daughter or son marrying through open marriage or these modern systems of marriage, which seem to be more common in the US, with a disproportionately high number of black attendees compared to the overall black population in the US. This raises questions about the correlation between what's happening in today's religion, spirits, and the experiences of black people.

Even though you cannot convince me that an Igbo Mum's girl or an Igbo Daddies' girl would turn to open marriage to find a life partner and forsake their own tribesmen, similarly, you cannot expect an Indian girl or a Jewish girl to shun their people and seek a match through open blind dating. Let us remember the biblical story of Jacob, Leah, and Rachel, and even Isaac, who was 40 when Abraham sent his steward, Eliezer, to Mesopotamia to find him a wife from his nephew Bethel's family. Eliezer chose the Aramean

Rebekah as Isaac's wife. We should not be carried away by civilization and advancements and forget to do things in the right way, as the devil sets people up in various ways particularly now tricks were discovered and bitterness is upon them.

Finally, considering the widespread prevalence of open marriages, mainly in the developed world, it's likely that the number of broken-up marriages will significantly increase in the next ten years. This is because the exposure of the spirits' tricks in our midst has led people to introduce blind dating to their lives based solely on physical attraction. For those who fall victim to this, the regret of a family breakup can be profound, significantly affecting not just the couples involved but also their children; please do reason this?

Similar spirits' tricks, that now the United States has confirmed that all countries in the world, in order to establish good relation with power, must accept same sex marriage women/women, or man/man? The devil is a liar.

Briefly, let I repeat it again, please we should not be carried away by civilization and advancements and forget to do things in the right way, as the devil sets people, societies and governments up in various ways, using those without human concern, particularly now tricks were discovered and bitterness is upon them.

Characteristic is here; right from the day I discovered the intentions of the spirits to mankind, that is the time I started killing them every day for years now. Do you know what? All the spirits (devils) that come with me from the day I departed Africa to Europe over 20 years now have killed all except Satan, one day I assumed to have killed Satan. Still, after coupled of days, Satan, through vision, reminded me how my Mother took me to one of our relatives when I was 6years Old. Satan did that to witness to me he was still alive and had not also been killed and out of fury, reminded me that spirits are not playing over any disobedient and that's why he reminded me how my Mum took me to one of our relatives on the day the family celebrated the joy of hairs cut of their 7years Old boy. That was born with ISI DADA. This is in my local dilates, meaning the guy was born with Raster hairs.

Consequently, Satan reminded me, and I remembered years ago, in my little age was there when almost my age mate celebrated his haircut and lots of children was invited, all kinds of dishes were served, and that is how it was in those days. These will be a witness to us all about the character of the spirits that are familiar to man, that when you want to know the mind of somebody to you, just one way or the other get the person upset, then sit back and watch his reaction, I mean what the person had in mind, whether good or bad. Because I have discovered the tricks of the unusual beings coupled with killing them, now Satan is not happy and opened up and reminded me of things that happened when I was a little boy and the consequences behind every disobedience.

I am here to remind us that spirits in our midst, the human opposition, are record-keepers, and they never let go; that's why the scripture said some modern people are still living in bondage through idolatry; these are the reasons the spirit's revenge. Now, even though tricks of the spirits against the living have been opened to all of us, and even if religion is no more today, the unusual beings are still in our midst; those things regarded as disobedient most still maintained because they never let go. So, the earlier we know this, the better for all of us. We need to educate ourselves spiritually because we live amid evil spirits, desperate and wicked against the living. Let people/Ministers set up spiritual schools?

Now, let's be completely open. According to the scriptures above, in those days, there was a time when a child would be born if the parents found out that the hairs of the child seemed with ISI DADA, which means Raster, according to tradition in those days. After nursing the child and during his upbringing, let's say when he will be around 3,4 or up to 6 years. The parents will organise a party, kind of, other children will be invited mostly for a witness, even food will be provided by the parents for the invitees, though, not a most depending on the parent's capability. And as regarded by the people in those days, after that hairs cut celebration. From that very moment, the child will start clearly seeing his destiny, future, and open doors. After that, as the child grows from that day, any other time the hair grows out, it will be cut off as normal, which will not require further celebration or inviting of people, and it will continue that way.

What is happening all over the World today? Well, the opposition in our midst is not after that; all they know is anyone that walks against; they will capitalise on that and take it up, and due to today's civilisation or development, people are now living life the way it pleases them without minding the outcome. Due to the wickedness of the opposition, any child with ISI DADA Spirits will do their best to block some of his/her destiny just due to disobedience. And they are there to comply. Anytime the person repents, his destiny may be revealed to him/her, and with more luck, doors will be opened unto him/her, too. I am here to announce that a large number of people have been unaware, whilst some were still aware of the topic raised. Many families eat from hand to mouth because of what the opposition is doing in their family just because of disobedience. And most of their destiny, future, or progress is blocked by the opposition. Spirits are experts in blocking or locking people's destinies. In many ways, spirits can attack you.

The person may be working hard, getting the money without knowing exactly how it has been spent, or they can make the person extravagant or even go from one end to the other without a proper reason just to spend what they have at hand. Did you know that some of these people with that style of hair, due to what oppositions were doing in their life some of them are just human beings and do not know are left or right? This is a proverb. Some Spirits will stir them to be rude in different ways, attacking them through taking all kinds of drinks, smoking, breaking up marriages, being uneducated, etc. Did you know spirits can stir an entire tribe to have that type of hair, just liken to a harlot? Spirits can set a whole tribe to practice harlots/prostitutes before any other thing in life? Just out of their wicked nature to destroy them.

Do you know that some men/women you will see with this kind of hair; you will nearly vomit what you're eating at that moment due to how dirt they appear? Because the devils have blocked their minds, even taking their minds off from washing their hair and bearing, month to month, on like a madman because the same spirits are behind it all.

Some people were not naturally born with that kind of hair. Still, due to bragging and raising shoulders, they started allowing their hair to grow and formed ISI DADA (Raster) on their own. These days' huge numbers of men are now making ways for devils to attacks them through their additions of life; I mean those men that tie their hair to compliment women. Did you know I have never witnessed that kind of hairstyle with a white man? Yes, I have been in Europe for a while now. Please, I have not said spirits left them behind. Remember the way spirits operate, that in a house of bondage, somebody may live, even if he is not involved in committing the Idol, but the person is living in the house of bondage with them, spirits do not count the person out; he/she is included, therefore, will receive the same punishments.

Like today's Ministers of the gospels, some Ministers are called into the ministry by the spirits, and at the same time, there are some other Ministers who called themselves (self-appointed Ministers) into the ministry; the spirits did not discount them; they all included praying and performing miracles, that how it is regarding what I mentioned above.

There are some guys with this kind of hair that the devils are laying eggs with and having issues in their hair without their knowledge. The type of people that the devil's con after having the long hair will at the same time put all in a bunk and cover it with a scarf; the opposition is desperate and wicked against any form of disrobing. Especially now their tricks are discovered, they are not happy, and sometimes, those guys with raster hairs look ugly when you look at their faces, though, their hearts may not be the same. Just because of those spirits in their hair makes it look ugly, and for that reason, any slightest thing you do with them, they get angry; some of them are very violent just because of those wicked spirits in the hairs and on their head.

Here are the latest these days: there are some parents that after giving birth, whether a boy or a girl, will decide not to temper with the baby's hair, just to allow it to grow out to use it and form it in any style they like, please do not get me wrong. Whatever has an advantage also has a disadvantage. Even though spirits are monitoring everyone, there are some big ladies/Men. If you see their long hair and how clean and shiny it looks like that of those in fashion shows, you may decide to get closer to them and know them better. Do not forget what I said. Once you decide to get out of the house of bondage, then clean yourselves.

After that, you will start to experience many changes and open doors in your life. All the doors devils have short against you start opening one after the other — I am not trying to kid you. I talk about experiences.

Through sleep, Spirits attack people; many local musicians have lost their lives on their way home from night concerts at their weakness; spirits stir the driver to fall asleep at the wheel, which will result in fatal accidents, mostly in third-world countries where the Motorway is wonderful. For example, are Nigeria local musicians late Celestine Ukwu, late January, a Nigerian local musician, died in a road accident after a night's concert; the Late Nathan Nwafor, a Nigerian local musician, also died in the accident with his groups. For this Late local musician, the promote sang a song asking, are we all Musicians going to die in an accident? I also mean, in the third-world countries, a good fraction of night drivers of big trucks has lost their lives through sleep attacks by the spirits world.

Selling of property or moving from your apartment to somewhere else? There is nothing that the wicked spirits in our midst does well than convincing people to change their mind. Therefore, before you do any of the two things mentioned above, please give a reason for it. Because too many have been shifted by the spirits unknowingly from where they are and what they had, and at last, they regret it. Remember, I have not said to sell your property or to vacate your house to somewhere else is bad, but try to give it time and reason it before commencing. Spirits in our midst are defined as stealing, killing, and destroying, which means they have nothing good for humanity. And they are 24hrs with you without the option of attentively listening to your thoughts and all your doing.

Harlots, if you accidentally find yourself using your body for money and want to stop it? Whatever addition you find yourself, spirits are behind it, and you can let it go. Is possible to let it go because it is transferable; very stubborn spirits, so you need to wholeheartedly stop it in this lifetime, but the decision is yours, so you need to decide, and if you completely made that decision, then the spirits behind it will allow you. But where can you find those spirits? You can find those brutal spirits in the clothes you wear, as little as they are, in the hairs of your head and inside your rooms. If you want it to stop so quickly, you need to be meditating on how spirits deceive people day and night; also, try always have gum/adhesive in your bag; anytime you think something stirs you to feel sexy, apply gum in your hand with the intent to rub it anywhere you feel like and always ready to share it with third party. I mean, if you seriously think about what I have said, in good conscience, you will seem very dangerous before those spirits, who, with speed, will negotiate somewhere else.

Madness: To witness the heights of the wickedness and selfishness of the spirits churches etc., worship.

Did you know that the spirits we worship in churches, I mean, the spirits behind entire world religions, are behind every madness seen around? This may sound unbelievable. Anytime you see a mad person, kindly look closely at him/her. You will be able to see small objects moving around him/her or within the hairs of the mad person, apart from those spirits that can be found in the clothes the mad person is wearing at that moment. So those small objects are the familiar spirits, the course of the madness, as they seem very brutal and do their best to destroy the mad person; that's the root of destruction, one of the jobs that defines the works of the Devils. Sometimes, when somebody becomes mad, friends, families or relatives will run around looking for ways to cure the mad person. Some people may decide to take the mad person to a native doctor, while others will look for other ways to get the man person healed. Even as they get the mad person to the native doctor, the native doctor understands quite well that it is madness, no matter the course. If the madman is violent, the doctor will have no option but to put the chain in his hand/handcuff. Then, after the charges are agreed upon with the sick family, the doctor will start work immediately by first gathering olive oil and applying all sorts of traditional remedies on the mad person. You find out that sometimes the sick person may stay with the native doctor for years, and still, the sick person does not know where he/she is. Sometimes, the spirits behind the madness may decide to reduce the numbers for deception. When the families visit the sick, the doctors will happily present the sick person before the family with the hope is getting better now than before.

Look? Sometime after the sick guy has been with the doctor for a couple of years, the spirits behind the sickness will completely keep off for further deception, which will allow the doctor to invite the sick's family with the point that he got far better now, so better now to take a sick guy home and advised them to be coming back to him every 2 weeks to collect further remedies and continuing treating him at home. Once, after a month or two, the family may have returned to the doctor for a collection of remedies. The spirits will come back again, and the whole sickness will start all over again, enabling the family to take the sick back to the native doctor the second time. Could you imagine the heights of the naughtiness of the spirits behind the entire world religion?

Could you believe that the sickness may continue with the guy to the point even the family will be tired of the sickness? Just because the natives' doctor did not, first of all, discover the pure roots/ sequence of the madness. Which made the spirits behind it not give up on the guy, and it continued like that, sometimes even unto the death of the mad person. Be careful here. I am narrating all this through experience. I hope you will not be surprised to hear that I was a complete madman during my time in the wilderness with the spirits, if not spray adhesive, I used to defend myself by killing them.

Therefore, I know what I am talking about. Just to announce to you, the spirits behind every madness are nothing to those who know them and know how to kill them. Consequently, madness can be healed in under three weeks to one month, no matter how long ago it started. Immediately, you raise what to use to kill them, and many of them will slip off and never come back because they do not like to be killed, and from there, the madman will start to gain himself. So, no matter what you are doing to heal a mad person without killing those spirits behind it, you're wasting your time, and those spirits are making a fool of you because they are spirits of ignorance.

The same goes for somebody possessed by evil spirits; sometimes, people are poses, and a Minister of the gospel will invite the person to the church for prayer. During prayer, you will hear 'devil, I cast you out' or 'come out from her in the name of Jesus' and the rest of it. But my question is this: where are you casting them to. As the Minister and the congregation will be screaming and shouting in the name of Jesus, the spirits, being very smart and clever, will just obey that name of Jesus for deception and pretend to have flown, but still hanging around, whilst some will be in the hairs and clothes the person wore. You may cast them out; they obey and fly to the person's house and wait for her there. Though no one is to blame, you can do anything without identifying your enemy.

Please, anybody that is possessed, the spirits behind it are those that from birth monitor the person for ages and not a different spirit. They can be found in the hair and the clothes the person is wearing at that moment, and if you want those spirits to keep off completely from that individual, go and buy spray adhesive, open up, speak it out, and even be ready to disclose to third parties how the spirits operate, tell them to keep off on you as simply as that. In good conscience, the stubborn spirits will obey you because they will not like to be killed and would not like others to know how they operate. So, that is the capital medicine to give to someone possessed, not by casting them out in the name of Jesus. Where are you casting them to, casting them out without killing them, within the time they come back again.

Listen, I am narrating these with experiences; I am a complete madman during the time of my wilderness with the spirits. On which the spirits were discovered to be otherwise. So, I know quite well what I am talking about. Glory to the company that made spray adhesive; that's what helped me so much to defend myself from the hands of these brutal, hopeless, and stubborn spirits. If not, I should have been dead a long time ago, and let me say it clearly, any Company in the World today that will first produce what it takes to kill off the spirits (devils) that have been monitoring human beings all these while without affecting human's life, Sky will be their limits. This will enable divorce, marriages, a nation fighting against a nation, Corruption, madness, family problems, and many more decrees to zero because of the same spirits behind it all.

In this chapter, consideration for these has been mentioned in my writing; I will give an example before I get to the main point. One Idolatrous priest who had been ministering in the shrine for so many years eventually, later the man died, and have got sons and daughters just to witness the heights and wickedness of the spirits in our midst. How they operate in the house of idolatrous priests, soothsayers, seers, and prophets, I mean, the way spirits start their operation in the house of those mentioned above after one or two years. If any of them died, then the spirits will revenge by attacking and killing the families; mind you, when any of those mentioned is alive ministering, all is well, but immediately, any have died. His children will be the next target before the spirits. Do you know the first thing the spirit attacks is their finances? The spirits will do their best to quench all the necessary way money is following into that family if possible. I mean, all the people in business in that family will start having one problem or the other in business until all goes out of business. Sometimes the spirits may start killing the man's family one by one through a road accident; all the intention and plans of the spirits are to ensure no human beings are left in that family, if possible, under generational curses to fulfil that which is written in the Bible that his children will be affected up to 3rd and 4th generation (*Exodus* 20:5) Spirits will be doing all these, for example-- the story of the children of Israel, as the spirits have brought them out from the house of bondage (Egypt) While on their way to the promised land, their where all killed by the same spirits. -the scripture made us understand that after the children of

Israel had left Egypt, some remained in the house of bondage (Idol worshipping). This means that disobedience is still ongoing up to this modern day. This is what I said before: when things are not going well around us, we need to find the cause and solution to it to stop it from progressing.

I am here to announce to you today that third-world countries are not doing well in all areas just because of the sins of our forefathers. The spirits in our midst are desperate and brutal in times of disobedience, and this is what is holding a lot of people in African countries unknowingly. Idol contaminations, for example, can be seen by going to Nigeria and witnessing the number of people who are using motorcycles for transport (Okada). I mean, 95 percent of these guys are former businessmen and women, and because of one thing or the other, they went out of business and ended up driving motorcycles for transport in order to nourish family.

I think have now been a while in the western World, but to be honest, have never for one day noticed or seen a white man's house where they have a shrine Idol or soothsayers, even though they may have but have not seen any. Please do not misunderstand me, not that there is none, but one or two out of 100. Surely, time has gone by since their forefathers were so many years ago. Still, today, they have forgotten about it. Today, Africans have clung to it, like they have almost abandoned religion, and Africa has taken over. Well, whatever has a start must also have an end, and this is the time for Africans to reason well about religion, so that is the bottom line for African sets back. On like in some towns and Cities in African countries, I mean, there are some towns like in Nigeria, if you hear the number of Idol shrines, soothsayers, seers, etc. they have within a town, you will be speechless. Did you know one thing about stubborn spirits? They may be because of the disobedience of a particular family, and the relatives will also be receiving the same punishments, unaware? Whether those relatives have been involved in the shrine or does not count, that is the character of the spirits. This is the reason one may have been born again for many years, but that punishment is still going after the person. Spirits in our midst do not reason like human beings; they never think back like humans, if not because of Ministers of the gospel, in order to keep the churches going, should have considered first before any other.

Africans, Third World, the facts have been discovered, and the time has come for a great change, but before that, the old way of life needs to be abandoned. I mean, to put away anything that will affect our 3rd and 4th generation because of our present lifestyle. The spirits

(devils) in our midst are nothing to somebody who has captured their tricks ways. Firstly, the spirits we are talking about can be killed in many ways because they take in breath like humans, so they die like every other living thing. But you need to decide, and when you make that decision, then the solution will come out. Could you imagine their wickedness? Taken human beings unaware as little as they are from the origin of man until now. I am desperate; please urge anyone who has set up any Shrine Idol, soothsayers, seers etc. Maybe your father, mother, uncle, or relatives, talk to them seriously to throw away all that has been set up because of traditions because the revenge is far greater.

Look, just to witness to us the way spirits reason and how they take action on revenge. Even if your Father, Mother or your brother has not set up any of the shrines mentioned above, it happened that maybe your relatives have set up one or somebody from the family where your Mother comes and it happens sometimes you pay them visits, and you were welcomed, anything they offered you there and you eat it, that's contamination, and that is it, you have been counted by the spirits. I don't know if what I said makes sense to you. The spirits can keep a record of things even up to 100 years without overlooking it; if you know how wicked Satan and devils are, you will even try to avoid going to a house or family that has any kind of Shrine, no matter the relationship, just to avoid committing yourself to the Idol, every means in their revenge. This is why third world countries were like this, due to the disobedience of our forefathers, and it is affecting a lot of people today unaware.

Now, let's talk about the solution because it does not matter to dispose of every image of Shrines and the rest of it. As you know, if you want to be a king, you need to prepare for war. Consequently, let it be known that putting away all the Shrine images is like going to somebody's house and parking all his belongings and putting them in the refuse. If you do, I don't think the person will keep quiet on you. This is a 100 percent sure of revenge. However, the most important is that you have discovered the spirit's tricks and have decided to do away with them. And as the decision has been made, the spirits are already shaking. Look, if I have not done what I asked you to do, I don't think I will have the chance to write all these down. I think I have classified all the solutions you need in these books, so do your best to go through all; I will stop it here to help me avoid a reputation.

Furthermore, it is quite understandable that Adam and Eve separated in the garden through the Spirit's conviction. A good percentage of divorced marriages are course through beliefs. Most importantly, any confirmed marriage that happened in today's church etc. Comes through spirit conviction. Some are favoured, while too many are not. ¾ of workers/drivers lose their jobs in the place of work done through spirit convictions. Also, today, all the highly intelligent men and women ministers of the gospels have abandoned their initial plans and have accepted the ministerial calling; some favoured while some did not. Why? Because of conviction, we know all the faiths who believe He is and also believe He is returning for the second message. Where all are accepted through conviction, so be wise of vision and the dream of nonentity living beings, which have not got much good for your future. Their works are defined as mentioned before.

The author, in his sitting room, meditating on the whole ISSUES OF the trail.

In this modern-day world, my question is this: "What is going on?" Well, I am not surprised because deception is a mighty weapon against novices. In this modern time, it is like any church that is not seen on Telly; does not belong. To the point, some of these preachers are seen in three or four different television channels in a week. If not more. Nevertheless, what I am pretty sure of is that throughout all the words in the scriptures, I have not seen the authorities talking about his Ministers appearing on Telly. Or let's assume that Jesus is real; during his time, did he appear on Telly? Besides, he did all the things that he did.

Again, the scriptures say that the Lord has known the end from the beginning. If so, he should have been able to tell that Telly station will be in existence. Still, all the same, so many Preachers do not know that these authorities are business merchandisers with degree qualifications called "tricks, cheating, and fraud." As the author of these manuscripts, who has been at war with these beings? I have noticed all the tricks, strategies, and plans these beings had in stock for 'today's faiths.'

These days, Christians and many others, the beings are taking all on-air vision. Do you know that a professional criminal once his operation is going on without interruption? Will keep on promoting the deal in different ways, to operate at a higher level. Previously, it was mostly Catholic seen on broadcast television. However, today, it is like every existing church is seen on television. However, preachers did not know that these authorities would prefer, if possible, taking everything on-air for them to keep spending their money without having much in their bank accounts. Spirits tricks are like any church that exists today. Within two or three years, their next target or vision will be to go on air, or the authorities will motivate/inspire the founder to think of buying or building their own church.

Which we all know that the consequences will fall only on the congregation members, or have you seen the authorities sending money from Sky/Heaven to the Ministers? Let me give you an example of what I am talking about that took place during this wilderness journey.

There was one Minister, who always put all the countries in which His church is broadcasting into their church bulletin, advising the members to keep focus. In African Countries, one in Nigeria, one in Kenya, one in Ghana, one in South Africa, in Europe, a couples of these in the

United Kingdom, one in Germany, one in France, and likewise in some States in America, and they must have had some in Asian countries by now. All the time, despite the collection of tithes and offerings, they will be selling bottles of Olive Oil, even to their Church Workers in every service they have to meet up, which is supposed to be given free to the tithes members for encouragement. So, if you calculate the amount that the Church is spending only on broadcasting every month, you will ask yourself what is going on in Religions.

The point is not that Ministers coming out on the television are bad, but it should not be the ultimate purpose of evangelism. Another question is whether the ministration appearing on Telex brings people to

the church or does it help some of the Faiths stay at home and keep listening to the gospel only from different networks? Well, if you understand the intention and the tricks of these authorities against the Churches. These authorities do not bother much whether people come to Churches through the television gospels or not. Still, all the things that the spirit wants are mostly for the Church to keep spending. Why? Because, if the church has enough money in their bank account, the founder may redirect the funds to/in a different agenda and couple that may also help the Minister to be reluctant in his/her ministerial work.

So by spending their money, the Ministers will keep running around to meet up. Well, I do not know if you have realized that these days, vast numbers of the Faith, mostly women (the Sisters) have decided only to stay at home praying with Family and listening to different types of gospel programs solely on the television?

Even to the point of making phone calls to their fellow Christians every week to get an idea of their Family prayer points and advising each order to make calls for prayers from different Ministers; from those ideas, both Families will organize a prayer meeting together with reference according to Matt18: 19. Also, within time, they set up a Prayer group, and from there, that will beget a Church. Along the line, that will be get another (a branch). Which will allow one of the Families to be the head? So now, both Families have gotten one Church each, and it goes on that way, with the excuse that the Scripture says, "Where two or three are gathered in my name (Jesus), there I'm in their midst."

It also says that if two of you on Earth agree on something, you ask for. It will be done for you by my father in Heaven. This empowers them from going to one church to listen to only on one man's preaching, and at the same time, will be paying tithes and other Church contributions as a member. As to how huge existing modern churches are setting up now, the same authorities are guiding and performing miracles and demonstrating power over them as time goes by. Though, most of the servants do not bother, because they mostly come out on telly to show up and compete with others so that people, friends, Families, and relatives can witness. Also, to see that their Church is doing very well, that will bring them more honour and respect.

Mind you that these authorities do not get tired in their business. Because that is all they can boast of. Once they see a new way of manipulation, they follow it up without delay. So what is in action for the beings these days is Churches buying their Church Buildings and taking all on-air vision. As we know, the money to be used will not fall from the sky (heaven).

These days, mostly in the third World Countries, even Soothsayers/seers are also coming out on telly for enticement because it is the same authorities in operation of which we did not know before.

To witness to you that the beings are business merchandise and do not waste time in getting new business once the old one is established. They go on negotiating for a new one. Just consider the way they have been taking the world right from the Ancient time of the idol priests and soothsayers to this modern time of religious prophets and ministers, stage by stage.

Both the faiths and the pagans keep calling and regarding the same beings without knowing their intentions and plans for humanity.

DATING SITES/ OPEN MARRIAGE

*I*n these modern-day Churches, despite collections of tithes and offerings, some Ministers still preaching and inviting people that is willing from all over the World. To sow seed/ donate into their Ministry through telly with the assurance that they use a highly secure payment system to enable you to make safe payments and donations online.

This easy and flexible solution allows you to make payments from various card schemes, which include Visa, MasterCard, and Verve. As to what is in action now, whether the person is religious or not does not account. With the promise, the god of a miracle will still reach you wherever you are through your giving. A miracle will manifest in every area of your life because you have sowed/given into His ministry. Despite this fact, the scriptures say that whoever does not confess with mouth and believes in the heart does not belong.

However, in the time of your giving into the Ministries, whether you believe or not does not matter. So, only novice Ministers will be preaching and were not invite people to sow seed/donate to their Ministry.

Furthermore, for the sake, religion is a great business. Both spiritual and self-appointed Ministers were under the same authorities. These made them accept all the people who have converted, maybe from Christianity to Islam, from Hindu to Buddhism, from Christianity to Hindu, and from Islam to Christianity, etc.

For these reasons, in all the sects of Faiths mentioned, very few among the Ministers are mentored and called by these spirits into the Ministry. While a vast number started Ministering to Churches as Ministers by defending themselves that God had already called them into the Ministry with the excuse they had ordained Ministers when they were with Pastor-A or Pastor-B. While some of them will tell you that the Holy Spirit taught them the bible for a couple of months or years and asked them to go and deliver his people. While others will give you so many reasons and excuses about why God has called them into the Ministry, and they were all welcomed by the beings leading the church because of deception and for the fact that they all belong to the same authorities. So, they were doing these because they knew quite well that we had been deceived.

If there is no deception, how could this happen on Earth? One Gospel Minister, I mean, it happened that after the man had married at a very young age and had eight children, six Boys and two Daughters. In the course, the Man had a calling in his life into the Ministry. Yes, and as he responded to the calling, within times, he started his Ministry. While his Children are growing day by day, likewise, the man and his wife are growing in the Ministry. However, after a couple of fewer years, they had their first branch of the ministries somewhere.

By the time they had the second branches of the departments, the man had already ordained his first son as a Minister. After a while of the new Minister helping the father in the Ministries, he set up his Ministry. In the course, after two years, the church had its third branches of the Ministries. The man likewise ordained the second son as a Minister as time goes by. As they are preparing to have their four departments. The third son of the Ministers was also ordered as a Minister and was instructed to be the Minister in charge of their fourth branch of the Ministries.

Within times, the first Daughter of the Ministers was also ordained as a Minister. After a while accompanying the parents in the Ministry, she went and set up her Church. Could you believe that Six Sons and One of the Daughters of the Man were all ordained through these ideas?

However, one of the Daughters decided not to get involved in the Ministry. If not, the whole six Male and two Daughters of the Man should have to be ordained Ministers. One thing I would like us to examine/realise is that sometimes you will see some dedicated members, Workers of about 40 to 60 years of age in a

Church for over 16,17 to 20years in particular Church who desire to become a Minister; nobody would like to ordain them as a Minister.

Again, sometimes, you will see a Son or a Daughter of a Minister who will be about 17 to 20 years of age ordained as a minister, and they will be allowed to stand at the pulpit ministering the gospel before the senior adults, very spiritual church workers and the congregation members. I do not know if what I'm saying makes sense to us? If not for deceptions, too many University graduates etc., and big adults in the church workers is supposed to be ordained Ministers and not just only to end up as a church worker.

Moreover, sometimes a founder of a church will call out 10 to 15etc., people from the congregation members. Pray and present them before the whole church and say that 2 to 3 days ago, these people were laid in his/her hearts to become church worker in their auditorium by the Holy Spirit. However, without the church realising, that is just a way to increase the number of steady tithe payers. Because you cannot be a worker in the church without paying your tithes, that should be disobedient and an insult to the Holy Ghost.

One more happening in religions these days is that this happened during the case in which these authorities' tricks were discovered. Could you believe, in one of these modern churches, the founders of the church, to witness to you the skills and the conviction power of the church authorities so it happened after a couple of fewer years, the Church is settled up. During that time, the church moved up and down, from one building to the other in the process. They did all they could and bought a property (two-story buildings); then, after two years of the purchase, the workers and some from the congregation joined to contribute one thousand Pounds each to pay off the mortgage areas of the very Church. After those contributions, the Church Mortgage was paid off.

However, the most crucial area I would like to point out is this that during the time this church is moving from one building to the other. Also, when the church is struggling for their monthly mortgage areas, the founders seemed very co-operates, calmed and holy before the church members. Then, after the Church mortgage has been paid off by the contributions of the Workers and some of the members, within times, the founders started showing up body language, bragging, and raising shoulders.

I do not know if you are following, which means, if any of the tithe payers (workers) willing to leave the Church to another, fine. Why? Because the church mortgage paid off. This also means that the church has no problem anymore. These are the characteristics of vast ministers of these modern churches of Holy Ghost. Very easy to discern among them.

Now, we can see that the conviction of the spirits is compelling; so far the beings are concerned, in times of tricks by which they use emptying the pocket of the faithful. These authorities do not struggle over this, very easy in what they can do. I am explaining all these, so we all will be able to understand all the tricks. Therefore, I consider it vital for humanity that deception of these authorities exposed for the freedom, liberation, and growth of Humanity.

If you serve me, I will bless your foods and your waters and take sickness away in your midst, the numbers of your days I will fulfil:

Okay, are all Ministers blessed? These days some ministers get married for numbers of years still without a child; today childless ministers are into child adoption. Ministers are into all kinds of eye problems using all kinds of glasses without a solution, these day's ministers are passing away through all kinds of death:

Greatest Mistake

None of these tapes above is gospel songs, but spiritual messages from different Ministers. These are what kept me focused during my time in the wilderness until the tricks are discovered.

Whatever, written in the bible, is the way humans have been living their lives. Also, the beings which cannot initiate much-imitated for deceiving us. I mean, the rod of Moses, the scripture talks about, is an example of the walking stick that mostly the seniors use (Old in age, elderly ones use) now and then. If you are familiar with the ancient lifestyles. Any rod that belonged to an older adult in those days represented his/her strengths. If something serious happened to any holder of the rod and the person got angry, he used that rod against you, smirked anybody, pointed the rod on you, and uttered some unusual words (a curse) against a name. It will surely come to pass because the familiar spirits are always within to act on the spoken words of the older adult.

As to show you how vital the rod was to the senior elders in those days to the extent that if any user of the rod died, friends, family, and relatives would do their best to see that the rod will be put into the person coffin before he/she buried. So they do not take anything of the elder's rod for granted. However, remember that it's all the same parables, idioms, and illustrations.

I would like us to answer this question. Do you believe that somebody will speak to the rock and water will gush out? The answer is no, but what the authorities are trying to let the faiths be acquainted with is about some disobedient ministers and the consequences behind disobedience. Another question I have is about how long do you think it took the Old faiths, right from the book of Genesis, where they started the journeys to the scriptures of Numbers, where they ended the travels with death?

Greatest Mistake

Even if you do not know, can you imagine? Let's reason this together, as it's written: the creator that destroyed most of his ministers and the entire congregations in the wilderness and left only two, Joshua and Caleb, how do you reason him?

Let me ask you, Minister(s), how many people among your congregate have you bullied (killed) since the history of your church or parents about how many of your children have you killed for going against your instructions? Because you are seen like the creator before them in the spiritual understanding, mind you that as it contained in the scriptures, we accept the creator to be more holy, loving, sympathetic, forgiving, and so on than humans.

Finally, in the real understanding of Moses, parables are ideas of letting the servants, etc., to be aware of spirit seriousness over instruction.

Yes, even though the promise was made, I'm sorry. After all, humans lie, and beings are imitators. Well, it will be well known; after all, they are spiritual beings. Suppose the entire world today decides to take action against these authorities for manipulating and deceiving us all the while. Well, in that case, I think, honestly speaking, they will be acquitted free because all the words that were supposed to have exposed the spirit's tricks before us were misunderstood by us — and also coupled with Less Interest of the Governments.

All this while the entire world is in the wilderness with these beings without discovering their roots.

Therefore, due to the cunning of the spirits, the mistake is the faiths understand it in a way that the authorities had spoken to the faiths in those days. However, be advised that from today on, most of the written words you see are illustrations of what will be seen in today's religions.

Meanwhile, even if such things happened years back, they're still happening now. Some ministers have passed away in our modern age, while some ministers are still alive. Likewise, some idol shrine priests have passed away, while some are still alive in this contemporary age. Some churches were even set up before the modern age, and later, because of one problem or the other, they closed down. At the same time, some are still going on now. So now, with this understanding in this modern time, the faiths the bible is talking about are present/right here on earth. So whatever you see that the beings did or said to the flocks in the Scriptures is a proverb illustration of what the authorities have in mind for today's age and not just only for the faiths, which also means Spiritual Israel. King Abraham and King David, who are the heads of all the Faiths in the Bible, are an illustration, like the Earthly Pope and the Archbishop of Canterbury.

Then the King as He is seated at his throne in Heaven with the son Jesus seated at his right hand as recorded, and all the inhabitants here on Earth are also an illustration of the Ancient Earthly king and his first son/messenger before his subjects. Then, Isaac, Jacob, Joseph, Moses, Matthew, Peter, Paul, and the rest of the Bible talked about are an illustration of today's Ministers of the gospels. So now, as we have gotten that right side of the revelation, we also need to get an understanding of the other side of it for proper digestion. Like the flocks, in the Scripture saw the land which the authorities had promised them before taking them into the wilderness, without getting into it. So are the heavenly pledges made by the same powers to the present-day religions, etc.? Which signifies the faiths that are dying today without getting to their holy promise?

Dating Sites/ Open Marriage

Then, He made us understand that only Joshua and Caleb had excellent Spirits. Who was qualified to enter into that? Promised Land? All these are given to us in parables, which means that the leaders of today's Religions, which are still alive, are leading today's Churches, etc., for the beings. These are also the reasons today's Religions are still matching because these authorities will not do without the use of Humans.

Mind you that these do not apply to Christians only, but also to other religions because they are the same spirits in leadership with the same tricks of promises. It was mentioned somewhere in the Scripture that Abraham was looking to see the land without noticing, and so are today's Christians who are also looking up, but all we see is just the sky without seeing that very Heavenly promise.

Hope you too, understand that the murmurings of the Old faiths in the wilderness are what is happening in today's Religions due to some difficulties, financial problems, and marital problems. For these, some of the faiths/people will be saying one thing or the other against the ministers. Because some petitions have not been answered, and some people may, even after confessing and accepting Jesus as their saviour for a while, still not see exactly their expectations.

Some will decide to backslide and abandon everything about religion and start life all over again as it pleases them. That's the reason the faiths complained, they said, that they should return to Egypt where they had been eating Fish, Cucumbers, Melons, Meat, and other stuff (Num11: 4, 5 and 6)

So whatever you see happen to the faiths in the bible/scriptures are examples (parables) of what is already happening in today's religion, the entire world at large, and this is what the beings have in mind to happen to today's congregates. However, due to the world civilisation, it's seen watered down a bit. All these expose the thoughts and values of the authorities the faiths worship.

Being Religious Or Not, The Stubborn Spirits
Not Count, They Monitor Everyone

Somebody I know, after a couple of years worshiping in a local church, looking for a lady to settle down with, the spirits made a promise to him in a way that caused a setback that nearly took his life, and in the end, it's all regrets.

Spirits deceives people in many ways; somebody may be sitting on a bus, aircraft, market place, in school, in the church, or somewhere else, out of a sudden, somebody sitting beside or next to you changes his/her seat, these are done by the spirits monitoring you in a way to avoid giving you help or good communications because they already know you are in need looking for help. Spirits move/distract people so easily, out of their wicked nature, without the knowledge of many.

Things Spirits Can Not Be Able to Do

As a Christian, any time I hear the word "spiritual husband", I will be wondering, trying to know and understand how it operates until it happened to me during this tribulation, and I discovered, as I have said, that is better to really know and have the full understanding of what one talks about before making meaning out of it. Some people say that <u>a woman with spiritual husband</u>, that will not have allowed the natural husband to make love to her if it happened that <u>the woman is married</u>. While some say that her spiritual husband will make her hate her natural husband, that's an awful wrong teaching, I hope you too know that sometimes people make up testimonies just for attention, self-esteem, and to stir people up in the church.

Now listen, in the whole universe today we have only male and female humans, and this is how it is with the spirits; male and female, and likewise with other animals which in origin are the ancestral spirits. They have been existing like every other living thing, so because of the knowledge of men and women of this age. Also, through the character, attitude, and lifestyle of these very ancestral spirits, another name is given to the spirits, which is the Familiar spirits, and at the same time, through the deception in the things of religion, these spirits are called Holy spirit by some sects of faiths called the Christians and the worst character of these spirits is jealousy Deut4:24. They are jealous of human beings, this is the reason they always like to imitate and copy humans in whatsoever we do.

These spirits meet women more than we can imagine, but not in some areas as some people preach or teach. I am sharing this with the experience I had during these wilderness periods.

In this passage, I would try my best to help us with some of the things the spirits heading the church could not do, which shows their limitations. Spirits beings (God) find it very difficult to kill human beings instantly. If not, I, the author of this volume, would have been dead long ago because right from the time their plains were known by me. Every one of their efforts has been without success. Even while asleep,

The mad people you are seeing today should have been dead long ago because they are the same spirits behind whatever they were going through. These are some of the reasons the spirits mostly kill people through accidents.

Again, in a place of work, to cause loss of job through conviction by using the person (line managers) in the position to do that is one of the easiest ways the spirits use to attack people in their finances. Suppose the person concerned has the full understanding of the spirit's ways of operation, even though they will do their best on that. In that case, they still will find it difficult, though depending on the individual, because that will be their biggest target, which they have tried countless times against me without success. This is because I really understand their ways. Spirit beings cannot be able to design or describe a baby in the womb unless the woman speaks it out or meditates about the practical sex in her womb. Then, the spirits around will hear it. If not, they are not able to say this is going to be a baby boy or baby girl; while the woman is pregnant, spirits are not able to do that.

Again, the spirit leading the church has no single power to make human beings conceive and become pregnant. I have mentioned this a couple of times. Women are being pregnant today through their husbands because that is the nature of every living thing (it's natural), and this is the reason you will be able to see some women after 1or 2 children; everything will cease (stop) while some will start again after some time.

Sometimes, some women will produce only male children and will be doing everything to have female child and vice versa without success. So that is the nature of every living thing; some women will get married for up to 5 years, etc., and still without any child. Sometimes, the man will start blaming the woman or the woman will blame the man. All these can stop, whether the fault is from the man or sometimes it may also come from the woman; it is our nature, so it is with other animals that are not the doing of the spirits. When things like this happen, it may not be the end of it. But I advise both couples to keep on having contact with each other. Many people have been through that, and later, something good happened.

Well, I'm sure you must have seen other animals, even to the point that some trees are also like that. For example, back home in my country, Nigeria, there was a mango tree; it happened that the mango tree was small at the time. It bears fruits, and after some years, it started bearing fruits every 2-year interval and do you know that this mango tree continued like that until it finally stopped while other ones that were the same age with the mango tree were still bearing fruits. So I am trying to point out that everything depends on one's nature, which no spirit or human beings have a hand on. And that will also show you the meaning of the life we are into.

Lastly in this passage, the spirits heading the church we are depending on is without the idea of what will happen in the next one hour let alone that of tomorrow if not by conviction. This is one of the reasons they operate mostly by giving visions and dreams, so whatever they say to you is a probability; that means it may or may not.

Right from the day I became a member of my church in 1997, and after a couple of 3 months, I was admiring two lovely Sisters in the church. So, as I was admiring, dreaming of having one of them as a dear one.

In 1999, this vision was shown to me, but honestly, I couldn't really understand the meaning until it was confirmed to me with some scriptures, even though I was still wondering and thinking how it would happen. The vision was shown to me in this manner, in a compound that was also revealed to me, and I understand it to likely be my new compound where I live in that vision. So, as I came out from one of the buildings in that compound, watching around, it happened that a tap in that compound started running out of a sudden to the point that outsiders were coming in with different sizes of buckets, fetching water from the tap. It happened that as those people started troubling one another, one of them tried to stop the tap from running but could not. After that, I went closer to them and told them to form a queue. After I had said that, my eyes opened in that vision.

After couple of days, (Genesis 26) was given to me in a vision, which says, in (Verse2) "Then the Lord appeared to him and said, do not go down to Egypt, live in the land I shall tell you. (Verse3) Dwell in this land and I will be with you and bless you, for you and your descendants, I will perform the oath which I swore to Abraham y (our father. In (Verse15) "now the Philistines, had dugged up all the wells which his father's servants had dug, in the days of Abraham his father, and they had filled them with earth.

Verse 18 says that "And Isaac dug again the wells of waters which they had dug in the days of Abraham his father, for the Philistines had stopped them up. Verse19 Also, Isaac's servants dug in the valley and found well-running water there.

So, in my understanding of those Visions and, the Tap running without control seemed to be my total well-being. And the people fetching the water seemed to be like in my business; customers buying and collecting their orders, likely sometimes customers have misunderstanding within themselves. The reason for the spirit's ways of operation is this: could you believe that the very two types of businesses that have spoken to me, as mentioned that I will go into after the wilderness, which was confirmed with (Isaiah45) was the very business that I dealt with back home which I have forgotten long ago and that is the character of the spirits; most of the time, that thing which you are familiar with, the spirits will steal that from you to the point that the person will never, ever remember it anymore; then he will use that thing to make it look like it was initially that way and these will also help us to know that the beings find it difficult initiating some new things on their own.

I do not know if you really understand my points here; the same trick was also used on Isaac in Genesis26:7 "and the men of the place asked about his wife. And he said she is my Sister for he was afraid to say she is my Wife because he thought lest the men of the place kill me for Rebecca because she is beautiful to behold".

Well, it's wonderful that most of the time, some of us Christians would understand scripture when it was preached, but not in the real sense of it, even to the point without knowing the true intentions of the spirits for that scripture will witness to you two more tricks of the spirits by given visions to me. In the process of this wilderness, there was a time when a vision was shown to me while asleep. In that vision, it happened that where I had lived for a couple of years in London, England, where every one of my properties was taken away from me. I was asked to leave the place by the police and the estate manager. In the process, my eyes opened, and right from that time, I was expecting, listening to the Lord, to say something about it, and there was no response.

Sometimes, I will be thinking it was the devil trying to mess my mind up at this difficult and finishing moment of the wilderness, and the worst part of it, at the time all these happened, there was nothing I could do anymore just because of the circumstances around me for the sake of the tribulation…

Could you trust that, as it happened where I lived so also it happened at the place where I worked. The place was also shown to me in a vision, and it happened likewise. I thought that was the different spirits of the devils trying to mess up my focus by showing me the two visions. But without understanding, that was also the very spirits that were encouraging me all this while this wilderness did that altogether because we were at a new stage in the wilderness and there was nothing I could do to prevent it because that was their intention.

They also knew that I was totally penniless in every area of my life, and they concluded that I would lose everything I had. So this is the point I made before the plan of the spirits for wilderness is to destroy. Just think back to what I have said concerning the children of Israel in the wilderness and what I mentioned about the present-day churches/religions, the vision of my place of work, and the furniture in my house where I lived that was shown to me in a vision. All of these are the way spirits laugh off in their usual way of making mockeries over issues.

In the whole universe today, we have only two types of humans being; male and female. Likewise, other animals and spirit beings have also male and female spirits. They are productive by lying on eggs. As a man will be able to drive a car, ride a bicycle, fly planes, and at the same time be able to teach in the college or wherever so also are the ancestral spirits in their operations. One spirit can make someone laugh or cry and also be able to make someone start having fear, etc.

Again, there is a Verse in the scriptures these authorities made great promises to the faiths and said, "If you serve me, I will bless your foods and your waters and take sickness away in your midst and the numbers of your days I will fulfil." Well, I do not know what you think about that verse, but I do know too well that ministers of the gospels are still full of needs in their lives, let alone other faiths.

This is one of the reasons that the faiths frequently ask in their daily prayer to give us that which you have promised us. Or don't you know if that verse of the scripture is sufficient as regarded and not for more attention? Lots of people in the churches today should not have any needs in their lives anymore?

Once more, my question is, if it were not for deception, what would the beings that made promises to you and me have for exchange? One Minister says that you cannot give what you do not have: these are the beings whose works are defined as stealing, killing, and destroying, and they are reproduced by laying an egg in the green grass, which means they have nothing rather than empty words that sound effect.

Okay, are all Ministers blessed? These days, some ministers get married for a number of years still without a child; today, childless ministers are into child adoption. Ministers are into all kinds of eye problems using all types of glasses without solutions. These day's Ministers are passing away through all kinds of death; what else are we to talk? It all means that if you do not work well, you will also not eat well. We are living in a developing world, in which we all have a short time, visions, dreams and promises, spirits' ways: The most painful deceits that have ever existed.

Furthermore, in one of the churches, a brother was given a prophecy to marry one beloved Sister in the same assembly. After both of the brethren had agreed on and gone into courtship, by the time both of them had concluded courtship, they agreed to marry each other. In the process, the mother of the man said no, that the marriage would not hold. When the news got to the faiths, both were very, very upset. Because of this, all of their plans are scattered. Everyone in the assembly was surprised by this because this was a vision of prophecy from the masters (the church authorities).

Then, it took one of them more than two years to get somebody else for marriage. We did not know what the authorities were doing before us because their ways of operation had not been exposed.

Other most dangerous weapons that the beings use to put people, congregations, or even the entire world in bondage are promises. So many people, ministers, congregates, barren women, particularly the single ones in the church today, are under one promise or the other from these authorities that are left unfulfilled without any reason. However, my question is simple. How can we believe in the things we have not witnessed rather than those things that we have seen with our naked eyes?

You may not understand what I'm trying to point out, but my point is: one of my pastors then, say "Use yourself as an example" So I'm here to witness to you that I'm pregnant with promises from these authorities right from 1998 that are still unfulfilled up to this date. One of the reasons for putting all this history in writing is unfulfilled promises from these authorities. The beings made some promises to me that made me go and make peace with my enemies to avoid any blockage and for the blessing to come to pass in my life.

How can you promise somebody, a mature man, that you will raise him as a millionaire in a local church assembly, and after many years in trail/tribulation and after the price have been paid, for the fulfilment to come to pass, then one thing or the other will the given as an excuse?

What I'm trying to let us realise is that promises of these authorities are the highest weapons of getting people's attention in things of the King. Remember all the promises King Joke made to the Tortoise in the land of Israel. Again remember all the promises he made to father Abraham in the bible. Also, remember up to 6 different promises that made to Jesus before bringing the message of his kingdom to his inhabitants here on earth.

Never in the history of professional liars will they operate without using promises that sound real or look effective to get that person or those groups of people's attention. Sometimes, the vision of prophecy will come to somebody in the congregation with the message that somebody in their family, maybe the stepmother, father, or mother-in-law, or that your big uncle is standing in your way/progress.

Sometimes, you will see something like the one I mentioned in the vision above. However, my reason is this: the very beings that are showing and pointing out your enemies in an image to you should have their names specifically if it is genuine spirits that are presenting those your enemies in a vision to you? Should have dealt with them first before your knowledge because you are supposed to be a son or daughter before them, as the scripture records. So be aware, all they are doing is for you to keep nagging, worrying, and not have rest of mind, and such are the pleasures of these beings.

The human's opposition and also such prophesy will make or motivate you not to be absent, which will help you to be more committed in the church activities. Or have you forgotten that the beings we are talking about are professional in times of tricks, and their works were defining as to steal, kill and to destroy?

This illustration is to help us realise that if not the type of the authority's concerns, I do not think that will be the best way of prophesying to his subjects about their future or something about their privacy. For the course, the congregation is full of different types of humans. However, do you realise the reasons why these authorities are doing all this mostly to the singles? It is to make it a bit difficult for them to marry as scheduled, and as I have said, such will, at the same time, help/draw a name to be more committed.

Anyway, some people still achieve in that area without minding what these beings are doing because such a majority has been a significant problem to many of the faiths. Without knowing or finding a solution to their problem, at the time, those brethren will still be tithing, including other Church contributions, without breaking through in some area of their problems.

ABRAHAM IS OUR FATHER

After discovering the spirit's tricks, the wilderness ended; now, as I prepare to settle down, one day, a friend of mine introduced me to a dear Sister who worshipped in one of these modern Churches. On the first day, I was invited to their Church; a very lively prophetic Church, and as I arrived around 8.45 am, the Church service was already going on. The Senior Pastor of the Church was ministering before the congregation. He was preaching, walking, and dancing in the midst of the congregation and with signs of pointing to some people for alter call and prophesying over them.

So, as I occupied my seat and within 20 minutes of my welcome, the Man came to me and asked me to stand up and with the prophetic message that the Lord ministered to him now. He said that he saw me in an open vision, with some tattered clothes on my shoulder, coming out of the pub. Also, concluded the message as madness, and everyone in the congregation was looking at me, and the Pastor later asked me to meet with him after the service for prayer. Then, the very Sister I was negotiating was also looking at me and was surprised, but I was not bothered because I knew the Spirits involved and how they operate. If you can still remember my past explanation, the ways the Spirits pass wrong information to Ministers against some of the people in the Church. So the beings that were walking after me right from the day I came out from this very wilderness, and as I have discovered their tricks, I have been aware that I wanted to settle down before exposing them.

Also, there were fighting against it. All I said now happened at the beginning of 2005. So help me to conclude this: let's assume you are in this position, and somebody that you are negotiating in a deep relationship hears this prophecy; what do you think will be the outcome?

More attention here, in a similar situation, happened in one of my friend's Churches, who invited me to their church to come and worship and also to look around in their

Church for the same purpose after I had come out from this wilderness, because after I had discovered the plans of these spirits. I stopped discriminating against Churches because all Churches are under the same leadership.

So, on my second visit to the very Church services, their Minister (A Prophetess) started giving prophetic words to the congregation, just about 14 of us. When the prophetess got to where I was seated, she said to me that God said that she should tell me that those things that are walking after me have decided that I will not make any achievement in life. However, the Lord has also responded to them on my behalf; they have not gotten the final say over my life.

The Minister also advised me to keep praying over it. Could you imagine the way beings operate? So this is another trick of letting the congregation know that this young man still has some problems, to expose me before these people (gathering) for single Sisters to keep away from me.

In 2004, between March and April, in London, England, in a prophetic church on one of the Tuesday evening prayer meetings. The Pastor (Prophetess) called me out before the congregation with the prophecy that last night had shown to her in a vision, where I was walking along with an ancient man carrying the older man's bag on my shoulder.

On the spot before the congregation, it was like the centre of the attraction before the congregation. She concluded the vision was a generational curse. Well, I did not know if you understand what that means. That's my very own Pastor, whom I had fellowshipped with for 6 to 7 years before this wilderness took place. She had also witnessed all the things I had been through in the desert for a couple of years.

She was aware that I had come out of the desert successfully. As now was the time to look for a future partner, and the Spirit still deceived her with a vision of my grandfather. Without remembering, they were doing that in a way to put off single Sisters in the Church in order to keep them away from me. Just help me to the reason this yourself? Do you know one thing that some Ministers Are?

Desperately, when dealing with some of their members, just because of that calling of the spirits upon their life?

Anyway, people in the Church were discouraged because of the ways prophetic words were given to them before the congregation. Could you imagine in one of the Churches, a massage of prophecy given to a Sister before the Church Workers? A vision of the Sister is shown, where the Sister uses her body for money in the city of London. It was like the Entire Sisters sitting in that Worker's meeting shrank under the ground for such a message before the Church Workers.

Also, the very Sister's concerns were not doubted; she was very shocked to expose her before her Pastors and fellow Church Workers. However, without the understanding that the Spirit guiding all churches is a gossiper, very mean against the living.

All the examples given is to let us know that, if not the type of the spirits behind the religions. I do not think that will be the best way of prophesying to his people about their future or something about their privacy because the congregations are full of different types of humans.

However, do you know the reasons why the spirits are doing all this against my marriage? It is to make it difficult for me to marry in that local church. Such must be a problem for many of the faiths without knowing or finding a solution to their problem. At the same time, those brethren will still be tithing, including other church contributions, without breaking through in some areas of their problems.

Sometimes, prophesy will come to somebody with the message that somebody in their Family, maybe the Stepmother, Father, or Mother-in-Law, or that the big Uncle is standing in their progress. Sometimes, you will see something like the one I mentioned in the vision above.

Nevertheless, my reason is that the very thing that is showing and pointing out your enemies in an image to you should be specific with their names. In my understanding, if he is a genuine spirit, presenting your enemies in a vision before you. Those Spirits should have dealt with them first before your knowledge because you are supposed to be a Son or Daughter before them, as the Scripture records.

So, mind you, all they are doing is for you to keep nagging, worrying, and not having the rest of your mind, and such is the pleasure of the spirits because they are jealous of you in all you are doing.

If you have considered it, you must have been able to deliver yourself from this very passage because I have classified these a couple of times. That is all I want you to know. No matter what anybody will be doing/sending against you, once the person is not doing that with his/her physical body.

Next, to be doing that, is the same Spirits that are giving you the vision of those people regarded as your enemies. Mind you, I have not said that is not possible. However, what I want you to know is not as assumed, maybe 5%, while the spirits are contributing so much of your negative thinking, helping you assume against those people. So while meditating over it, then, they are also there with you 24 hours a day helping you do that, and such are their pleasures.

In these very passages, I will do my best to make the reasons very clear for us to understand. Firstly, we have discovered the authorities behind the entire religions and also have a bit of an understanding of what they can do and what they cannot do. Here are most tricks of the beings in things of religions.

They find it difficult to direct single ones in the congregation to who their spouse/life partner will be, and this has contributed to the life of so many single ones not getting married as scheduled. That's because the beings are jealous of humans getting married. As I was in the church then, for a couple of years, as a born again Christian, without sex and while praying and waiting for my bible Rachael (life partner) to come, then I realised that what I'm saying mostly happens to those that are not yet married.

If you have listened, you must have been able to deliver yourself from this very passage because I have earlier classified these a couple of times. All I want you to know is this: no matter what anybody will send to you, once the person is not doing that with his/her physical body or using somebody else. Then, the next to be doing that on their behalf is the same spirit that will motivate somebody to do that. Mind you, I have not said that such is not possible, but what I want you to know is not as assumed, but maybe 5%, while they are contributing so much of your negative thinking, helping you think against those people, so while thinking about them. The beings are with you 24 hours, helping you meditate on unnecessary assumptions because such are the pleasures of the wicked.

In a real sense, even the way some ministers used to receive a prophetic word from these authorities, sometimes seeing unusual, how could creator be giving a message through the apostle in a local church assemble to good numbers of people in a congregation at a sitting? If you witness, you could notice most of these messages, likely to be what somebody, your human enemy, or the devils (spirits) have done or are trying to do in your life.

Sometimes, the ghosts will whisper to the preacher to say to his/her congregation. Nevertheless, because of who I am, I, the Lord, will avenge, and after some people have received such prophetic words, I kept on meditating on that. The very spirits that are in charge/monitoring will also help the person in doing that, and sometimes, the person involved is seen as confused over some issues without understanding that every prophetic word of these authorities is under probability.

Likewise, even if without those prophetic words, that thing or those things will still also be 50/50, it may or may not happen. Remember, the same life afflictions apply to non-religious and free thinkers, yet they are achieving success moving on in life. If not, ministers of the gospels should have long ago started doubting the manipulation of the spirits through some of the unusual prophetic words frequently given by these authorities before the congregations.

Now and then, some Ministers lie coupled with tricks to get through in life with the reference that Abraham lied Because of Sarah, his wife (Genesis20:2, 12:13)

Keep in mind the way it is explained. Visions and dreams have been given to us by the authorities in our sleep. I do hope you still remember that King Job's suffering in the bible represents a present-day Minister who is sick while even in the faith.

Then again, this also exposes ways the beings have been making fools of humans while we are asleep. Let's refresh our mind on this: the proverbs vision from the spirit to King Nebuchadnezzar, which was explained and interpreted to him by King Daniel (Daniel 2: 14). Again, somewhere in the scripture, it says that vision will only come to pass according to the time appointed. Do you know three- quarters of the messages given to Ministers of the gospels by these authorities are through visions and dreams, as they received it and shared it before the congregation? With an understanding of the beings, that was also the way scriptures were written through the writers, so not that the spirits were sitting down with them (writers) at all times talking to them.

Again, to witness to us, visions and dreams given to us by the spirits are also in proverbs and idioms. It says, "The multitude of all the nations who fight against Ariel. Even all who fight against her fortress and distress her shall be as a dream of a night vision." It shall also be as when a hungry man dreams and look — he eats but awakes, and his soul is still empty, or as when a thirsty man dreams and looks – he drinks. However, when he awakens, indeed, he is faint, and his soul still craves, so all the multitude of all Nations shall be, who fight against Mount Zion (Isaiah 29:7). Please give it a reason, reader.

When I have not found out their tricks, any time I have a vision, I will wonder how my image witnesses me in a night vision. Sometimes, I concluded that nothing is impossible with the Lord; well, maybe somebody else may wonder as I did. Nevertheless, as I have said when you're asleep and you have a vision or dream.

It does not mean that whoever is showing you that vision has your picture or pictures of those things at hand before that could do that. Well, you will see some of those things/

messages in a vision as an image because you're at sleep. The beings will be whispering into your ear during your sleep, and you will see and hear the echo that way. If the beings want you to see a picture of any image in a vision, the very Spirit who will be whispering into your ear will mention and describe the picture into your ear. You will be seeing/witnessing what the Spirit has said as a picture image in that vision while you are asleep.

If it happens, the beings concerned will communicate with you verbally while you are asleep without showing you any vision or picture. That means dreams. In this case, the beings involved will just be whispering into your ear, and you will be dreaming the echoes as/in a dream and nothing more. Keep in mind, all the beings involved were those familiar spirits that have, for ages, been following and walking after you from your childhood. Those who know you in and out that read and understand your inner mind. Any spirits without your history or who are not familiar with you cannot do that.

Listen to this; it may sound funny. Can you believe at the time, I was taught by the spirits how to study the bible and was also able to understand the visions of the Spirit for this very wilderness? At the end of 1997, the first vision that was given to me by the Spirit was a vision where after I had finished the day's work. While I was walking home, a night vision showed me that two different spirits were also walking after me. I recognized the first one in that vision as the spirit of the Lord Jesus, and I even knew the second one as the Spirit of the Devil.

Can you trust that in that vision, as I saw the Spirit of Satan also walking after me, I immediately called on Jesus to witness Satan walking after me? In response, Jesus said to me in that vision that I should stop calling on Him, that He has given me the power over Satan. However, I understand that if I allowed Satan to keep walking after me, I would be the one to lose. So after He responded, then I rebuked Satan using the name of Jesus according to the word of God in Jude 1:9. The wicked one flew immediately, and my eyes opened after the vision.

I hope you have seen how cunning the spirits are, manipulating the faiths all these while; 2 different spirits.

One was recognized as Jesus and the other as the devils/Satan, while both were the familiar spirits that had been monitoring me for ages, and they planned to use these two spirits to deceive me in that vision. Even though significant, the visions given to me before the tribulation helped me so much understand the Spirit's tricks amid this tribulation. Mind you; they were doing all this because they had initially concluded that I was going to die in the wilderness. Can you remember the reasons for those spirits' tricks? In that vision, I turned back, recognized the devil, and rebuked him in the name of Jesus. He flew away. As the Spirit pretended to have departed, still, those very spirits were at the same time hanging around walking after me.

That precisely the way the spirits have been operating in the churches, mosque etc. I do not know if you understand spirits tricks? So, what I would like you to know is the death of the children of Israel.

SPIRIT WHISPERS

In the bible, it has concluded that even before taking them into the wilderness. My survival will also help us to know that the spirits do not have an understanding of the future. If not, they should not have done some of the things they did before taking me into the wilderness. Nevertheless, they teach us spirits' way of maltreating men and women of this age to fulfil what is written in the bible. Whatever vision or dreams the spirits have given to you today, there must be a reason for doing it. It may be for good, which I reluctantly give 5%. It may be for evil, which can also offer 25%.

Also, mostly, it may be to use the vision to put you off from where you are going, and at the same time, it will also look real before you, which I would also give 70%.

Why? How can a nonentity spirit give you a vision of your future or whatever, and it comes to pass? The Spirits that are giving you night vision of your prospects have nothing on their own, and the scriptures define their works as to steal, kill, and destroy. Again, the Spirit that is giving you a vision of your future does not know what is going to happen in the next 1-minute if not by their conviction of which they are not 100% sure.

Whatever vision or dream the spirit behind religions is giving you today is under probability, which means they are not sure of the outcome of the revelation. That is one of the reasons it said in the scripture that vision is for an appointed time, and when the time comes, it will speak because the spirits have no exact time of the manifestation. These are the reasons they find it difficult to be specific in whatever they are doing amid the faiths.

An appointed time that the vision will speak as recorded in the scripture, and so many of us did not understand that appointed time is a deceptive word. Appointed time without being specific equally means no time.

That may also mean that it can happen now, tomorrow, or next year. It may take years to come to pass. Is that the way God should operate? After all, Abraham and his wife Sarah waited for nine years to have their only son, Isaac. Then, mind you, this is a proverb/adage of the spirits to the faiths, not in a physical manifestation. Still, very many of the flogs, mostly the barren women, lack that understanding while putting all hope in those words.

Word says that Adam lived for 930 years, and he died; Seth lived for 912 years, and then he died; Cain lived for 910 years, and he died; Noah lived for 950, and he died. Enoch lived for 365 years, and he took him. Again, Elijah went up by a whirlwind into Heaven. As recorded, it further says, "Because of sin, he decreased the days of Man. That's spirit's ways of boasting, as you/I can self-praise far more than these authorities of the Entire World religion,"

Moses, stretched out his hand over the Sea, and the Lord, caused the Sea to go back by a strong east wind all that night and made the Sea into dry land, and the water was like a wall to them on their right hand and their left: what is happening today regarding the ocean flood, scripture says he created the Ocean and gave it boundaries where to stop? (Psalm 104:9) that's spirit's ways of boasting.

Greatest Mistake

These are used daily for many years for evangelism across London, Peckham, Dalston, Seven Sisters, Woolwich, Camberwell, Lewisham etc. I was using these bibles to deliver the gospel of the Kingdom

Self-praising is one of the secrets of professional liars; the beings can self-praise before you in a way for you to believe whatever you may have told. Let's look into the scripture for some examples; He says, "Let not your heart be troubled: if you believe in me, also believe in my words. In my father's house are many mansions; if it were not so, I would not have told you. I am going to prepare a place for you. And if I go and prepare a place for you, I will come again and receive you to myself, that where I'm, there will you may also be." (John14:1-3)

It's one self-praise of these authority spikes many of the faiths now and then to be in bondage unaware. My question is this, how can these beings live in a mansion? Okay, these beings that say all these, now, we have discovered that they existed here on Earth. Have they had any estate here on Earth? The answer is no. Therefore, because of the tall mansions we have here on Earth, the beings imitated them for more attention.

Deception is powerful;

Boasting of the professional liars is this, which says, "And Moses said to the people. Do not be afraid, stand still and see the salvation of the Lord, which He will accomplish for you today, for the Egyptians whom you see today, you shall see them no more forever" (Exodus14:13-29). The Lord will fight for you, and you shall hold your peace. Then He said to Moses, why do you cry to me? Tell your people to go forward.

Greatest Mistake

Nevertheless, lift your rod, stretch out your hand over the Sea, and divide it, and your people will go on dry ground through the midst of the Sea. I indeed will harden the hearts of the Egyptians, and they shall follow them so that I will gain honour over Pharaoh and all his army, his chariots, and his horsemen. Then the Egyptians shall know that I am the Lord when I have gained recognition for myself over Pharaoh, his chariots, and his horsemen.

Then Moses stretched out his hand over the Sea, and the Lord caused the Sea to go back by a strong east wind all that night and made the Sea into dry land, and the water was like a wall to them on their right hand, and their left and the Egyptians pursued and went after them into the midst of the Sea. Then, all Pharaoh's horses, his chariots, and his horsemen. Then, He told Moses to stretch out his hand over the sea and that the water may come back upon the Egyptians.

On their chariots and their horsemen, Moses stretched out his hand over the Sea. When morning appeared, the sea returned to its full depth while the Egyptians were fleeing into it. So then He threw the Egyptians amid the Sea. Then, the water returned and covered the chariots. The horsemen and all the army of Pharaoh that came into the Sea after them, not one of them remained. However, the faiths had walked on dry land amid the Sea. And the water was like a wall to them on their right hand and their left hand.

Listen to this. Do you know one problem in the lives of professional liars? Lying has become part of them. Lying is in their bloodline, which is transferable. So, whatever comes out from them is a lie. They will be saying anything that comes into their minds without option because of their nature. Also, as the ancestors involved have already been deceived at first, remember, according to bible understanding, the Egyptians and the Army of Pharaoh equally mean devils or the enemy of the Creator.

While the beings that inspired the bible are behind it all, so it would help if you reasoned these very passages of my explanation yourselves. Some mature faiths regarded the rod of Moses as Jesus Christ, and this is the reason they believed that He did miraculous things with the rod through Moses, without the real understanding that all imitated humans' ways of doing magic here on Earth. As stated above, we need to realise that water, standing like a wall before the Children of Israel passed through it, was imitated from the Ocean waves here on Earth, which is the nature of the Ocean, and it is still in existence up to these days.

Deceit is like a growth factory:

In these paragraphs, I have only two things to bring to our attention: the way it works. I will, first of all, give you an illustration of a growth factory. In the world today, there are so many growth factories. In the field of a growth factory, there are also so many things involved that cannot be handled by an individual. Though, the factory may have grown to the point that one person cannot feel it. Still, at the time, the factory was set up. One person was able to handle it.

Yet, because the factory has grown, it attracts many people, customers, and companies as well. A growth factory may have started in one country. Due to its production and their efficient management, it started expanding with so many branches within the very land it first launched because the factory was not reluctant to do business, the management started thinking of expanding the business to other countries.

By the time they know it, the Company has got many branches in different countries. In the process of these, you found out that the growth factory has expanded to many other Countries to the point a name would find it difficult to know where it first started.

However, the point is, why will a factory be doing exceedingly well even to the end of having branches and franchises in other Countries? Well, for the fact the Company's products and management are well. Also, they were very disciplined in business, which is enough for the growth of the market. This is enough to attract other people, local traders, companies, and franchises to come to them for their products.

That means that by the time a company will grow to the point of having a franchise, that means the Company is doing exceedingly well. You will find out that when a Factory/Company has no problem with raw materials for production, the growth of that factory will be at once because the raw materials are always there for producers to make use of it. In a factory like this, the suppliers of the raw materials will frequently make phone calls, knocking on their door to supply them with natural materials.

This kind of growth factory will only start collapsing when it starts lacking the attention of its raw material suppliers. When such happens, it will first affect its franchise, and as time goes on, if the factory is still out of the raw materials and the managers and directors do not know what to do about it. The next people to be affected in the growth factory are the extended branches.

However, if the problem is still there, then, it will start losing its customers, and if that continues. Some of the offices will begin closing down one after the other because the kitchen is unable to supply them with goods anymore.

Also, if after closing down all the extended branches, the factory problems are still there, then it will start affecting some of the managers, who will lose their jobs. There will be a time when, even in the very place the growth factory first started, staff will begin losing their jobs because the factory is experiencing problems of raw materials, which make them unable to produce goods any longer. If the issues are not solved within time, the growth factory will stop producing the products entirely.

VISIONS, DREAMS AND PROMISES, SPIRITS WAYS

These days, many factories have been out of business because of mismanagements and not having adequate raw materials for the production of goods in a factory where they lack raw materials. The management will find it very difficult to excel. When it happens, the company will have no alternative but to close down the factory just because it does not have raw materials for the production of goods.

Again, in these paragraphs, I will do my best to give us an illustration of what deception is like. Anyway, I do hope you understand, too. Nevertheless, this is the way I see the word fraud. Listen to this, in the early 70s in one of the countries in Africa, when we heard of all the happenings in the advanced countries, there were very few who travelled abroad than to the extent many people were dreaming of going abroad, because of what people had said. Whenever a name was travelling abroad, it seemed like someone who was going to Heaven, let's assume.

Sometimes, you would see families after escorting any of their family members travelling abroad to the airport. By the time the person is about to check in, some of the family members that accompanied him/her will start crying if the person will not come back or will not be seen anymore because of the kind of life in the Western world as we have told.

In those days, many believed that the Western government paid everyone monthly. For these, the societies were living very well whether you were working or not. In fact, the Governments are not weak and have provided almost everything for the nations, which made some people not to be working for their daily living. We have been told that machines do nearly all the work for them, and that's why their complexion (the colour of their skin) is immaculate all day.

Visions, Dreams And Promises, Spirits Ways

Their skin seems very soft because they are not involved in daily jobs, and machines do everything. For these, many of us were deceived, dreaming of going abroad where the Government would be feeding everyone, that all one needs is to comply with the laws, sitting down at home watching Telly, listening of the Government's news, and reading the Newspapers.

However, all sorts of rumours were going on then because some people wanted to be successful without working or being involved in a secular job. One characteristic of humans is that they know how to spread and broadcast fake news just for self-esteem. You find out everything within a short period as the story reaches everyone. So, during this time in the 70s, going abroad seemed to be the ultimate choice. Just because of a deceptive word that had ministered, maybe through phone calls or through some people who had been to the advanced world and came back, made up news before friends and families, and from there, the news spreads.

So, it happened after a while; some people have travelled and come back, sharing their experiences with examples. That before a German Lady was able to have you as a close friend. She would first of all like to know what you are doing for a living. I mean your job, your occupation, and now, the news also spread everywhere.

Some people were very shocked to hear this, and people started saying that the Western world is not as usual, that everything has now changed, and since then, people have come to discover all the bad news. These days, people ask me what is happening; what is the story about the western countries today? I can now tell you that today, there are high numbers of people you would offer sponsor to go and live abroad.

They will turn it down because it now seems like everyone has been exposed to the things/happenings in Western countries, which is not made for lazy people who do not want to be involved in anything. Yet, I still want to be rich. So, people have now realized that the Western world is not as they have been taught. So for these, today, many give second thoughts on going to live in a world of the West.

However, surprisingly, one church was established by a minister from one of the African countries in the year 2003 in London, England. Where the spirits discovered to be otherwise, you may not believe that this assembles, despite the regular services, making it a duty of having deliverance meeting for 2 hours. Each day of the meeting, Monday to Saturday, and very many of the attendees are women. After a couple of days at the church, I got involved in the conference, though I later decided not to continue. I instead kept waiting on the King to fulfil that which he had promised me before this wilderness. After the experiences and the kind of spirits involved, I found out it was all empty promises, and that was where the desert ended in the year 2005.

Again, in this assembly mentioned, the deliverance meeting had been going on there right from the history of the church. As the Minister explained, right from the day he was called into the ministry, he was told by the authorities to go and deliver his people/subjects and the Apostle being a good servant and very obedient to the master, and did not want to disobey the King, and deliverance meetings have been going on ever since the history of that assembly, not only in his first church, but in all of his branches because deliverance is the foundation of his ministries from the masters, he said that no matter what other ministers are saying against his church, he will keep that word alive, doing what the King has told him from the beginning.

Any time the deliverance meeting was going on, you would be able to hear congregates shouting, "Devil, I cast you out in the name of Jesus." Come out from her in the mighty name of Jesus and all other words. While they are doing that, those beings monitoring each one of them, as usual, will be on a break, waiting for them to finish and come out. Though, is like they pretend to be running away from the angels of God as the faiths believed. However, the point is, as the believer casts out the devils, do they die or is it just another way of deception? The answer is no; they will only obey the name of Jesus for that very moment and keep off, just for deceit, and at the same time, keep hanging around because they operate in two ways.

Do you know the beings are making mockeries of those faiths? Especially the women by using old members in the church to bring other women in a way for the church to keep casting out the devils. Without understanding that it's a waste of time that the authorities do not deliver anybody. By the way, in what sickness or problem are the authorities providing them?

Is it from stroke, convulsion, breast cancer, or for the people that are looking for the fruit of the womb? These are the authorities by contradiction that is well known for stealing, killing, and destroying that was born and brought up in the green grass.

They are human opposition. Spirits cannot even heal a headache, unless somebody that is possessed by the same beings, then when somebody with spiritual authority prays, they may pretend and decide to let go. These Sisters mentioned will keep attending deliverance meeting yet waiting for miracles to happen, all that is deceit. The scripture says that on the last day, many shall be misled.

In this chapter, I will do my best to explain to us how foolish we have been before the hopeless beings. When we mention the word "deceives," it merely means conviction and disappointment, making you believe on what you have told and taking you out of that which you may have already known by making you accept on what is false. The button line is to mislead.

It may be from where you got involved. It may be in your business, and you may have been disappointed by somebody. It could also be in your marital life or what you believed. Or it may be that spirits have used a close friend to Minister to you. Lots of people now and then have been disappointed in one way or another, and no human being living under the sun will say that he/she has never been disappointed or misled by something.

For example, a friend of mine here in London-England trusted a Minister who was travelling from London to Nigeria. The guy gave the Minister some money to give to his mother in Nigeria to solve a severe family problem.

When the Minister came back from Nigeria to London, the guy did not bother to ask the Minister how the message went because he had every trust that he had delivered the message to the mother. However, amazingly, after one week, the Minister had come back. The brother called her mother on the phone, and he found out the Minister did not deliver a message to the mother. The guy went and asked the Minister, and he told him that he was unfortunate. The money was diverted because of some problems. It took him 3 to 4 months to repay the money. Well, the guy regretted it.

So, disappointment seems to be part of us because no one is perfect. However, at least human beings have got the sense to reason correctly, but some people are not making use of it. As the reason when we are disappointed over something, we try the possible way to come out of it or reverse from that in order not to continue again with the same mistake. So, the type of deception that caused disappointment we are going to look into is the disappointment in the hands of these authorities we have regarded as our Creator.

PROFESSIONAL LIARS -

All the worshippers, no matter the sects you belong to and no matter the kind of name you give to your Creator. Still, they are all the same spirits. Well, I do not know about you. These are the types of disappointments I experienced with the beings over what I have been taught. Recall that we are still on the topic of. *"<u>Deceives of Professional Liars.</u>"*

Let's look into the scriptures for more evidence. Well, I will, first of all, give us an example of how the authorities deceive the Ministers because they first cheated before the flogs and the Entire World. In the year 1999, in London-England, one of the Apostles then shared with us how the authorities showed him/her three young men in a night vision while asleep on their way travelling from one of the African countries to Brazil. The King advised the

Minister to pray and command those three guys to go back to Africa. However, the Minister did not know the reason. Also, the facial look of those guys was not familiar to the Apostle. Though the Minister assumed that they must have been drug barons, the Minister did obey the King. Then, on one of the nights, the Minister prayed a very fervent prayer and commanded those guys with the power the King had given to him/her. Those guys in prayer went back to the Africans that the King was not with them on that journey.

Then, after the Minister had done that, after around four weeks, the King showed the Minister those three young men. Minister prayed for in a vision, where they had gone back to their country of origin of that prayer. So, for these reasons, the Apostle was happy, and that made the Apostle share it before the assembles.

However, the Minister did not recall the previous month before the King gave the vision of those guys. All of her preaching and teaching before the church were about how young people these days are disobeying God and not doing the will of God.

For this reason, by the time the mind of the Minister was out from that gospel message. Then, the spirits came up with the vision of the three young men travelling to Brazil from Africa before her. Just in a trick way to witness to the Minister and the congregates that what the Minister taught the assembles the previous month is proper.

Being's tricks and deception are compelling. The fraud is this: the authorities of the religions we are talking about, apart from conviction, are not able to know or see what is going to happen in the next 1 Minute qu. I have mentioned this a couple of times. What I'm saying is that these authorities have no power to tell somebody in England. What is happening in Africa instantly, at a particular moment unless somebody just came from Africa to England and the spirits that are living in England will now be able to gather some new information from the very one that came with a name from Africa. Then, they can exchange current information.

I want to mention this, though. It seems a bit different from what I have in mind for this passage. However, to witness to us how these authorities operate before the congregation. Apart from what is written down in the Scripture. They mostly capitalize on the thoughts of the

Ministers and carry out whatever they are doing before the congregation. Mind you, we are exposing the works of the opposition; I'm not trying to put anybody down or to undermine. At the same time, it is what we are experiencing in the church, etc., and around us. That will be used to expose the opposition.

Another trick of the beings that looks frightening is this: one man of the gospels shared this with us after he had finished a lesson with his bible students. The topic was how to develop faith in your Creator and how faith works. While teaching the students in the class, the Apostle was doing their best to witness students what faith is all about and how it works. He asked one of the students to bring two small plants of leaves before the students in the class. Then, another student was asked to bring two cups in a way to put manure right inside, and after they had done that.

The Apostle stood before the students and put each of the plants differently in the cups that had manure. He then declares/speaks a curse on one of the plants and also maintains a blessing on the second plant in the other container.

He said to the students, "The cup plant which he pronounced with a curse will first die, while the other cup that is marked with a blessing of the King will live because of his faith. And the way to show/witness students the power of agreement and the power of spoken words that come out of our mouth."

After saying these, they all agreed. So every morning, before having the daily lesson in the class, they would utter curses on the plant that was pronounced a cursed, and utter blessing on the cup was marked with a blessing. While doing these, they will be watering both plants, but after a while, the plant that was cursed withered and died while the one pronounced blessing was alive up to the time they wanted.

My point is such an illustration of how faith works is not enough to convince somebody how faith works. However, we have discovered the powers behind the religions. If not, to get the plant killed within an hour is very easy compared to what the Spirits we are talking about are capable of doing. I mean, the authorities kindly allowed the cursed plant to stay alive for some days to deceive the Minister and his students that faith works. Instead, the spirits can keep coming together, stepping themselves on the cursed plant every night to make sure that it dies within a day.

It is effortless for them to do that. However, if the King is real and his servant uses such an illustration of how faith works. I think that will be an insult to the Creator after he has created all things, instead of using something more serious or bringing a dead body from the mortuary if you do not mind and pray so that he can prove that faith works. Or to pray for rain to fall for at least one month. Suppose it was true that Elijah in the bible prayed and there was no rain for three months.

What else are we to talk about? If the beings can make humans run mad all the days of his/her lives without recovering, how much more for them to get small plants to die instantly? These beings are behind it when a minister prays for somebody. The spirits will immediately motivate the persons in their usual way, and the person will see himself on the floor, and the congregation will marvel or be amazed at the power without knowing it is the works of the unusual beings.

"Mind you, we have to expose devils, and we will not only use the things that happened in the time past to do that.

Nonetheless, what happened in our present time in a way to give examples of the manipulation of these beings?

It says that in the Olden days, Idioms and Proverbs were like the sauce the ancestors used to eat their food. So the words of proverbs, idioms, etc., were very rampant in those days. Still, we, the modernists, due to today's civilization, do not have that kind of understanding, and the beings behind the religions have no choice/option but to continue making a fool of us through beliefs. That will also teach us the value of life, which we are.

(Isaiah 2:2-3) Says, "Now, it shall come to pass, in the latter days that the mountains of the Lord's house shall be established on the top of the mountain, and shall exalt above the hills, and all nations shall flow to it. Many people shall come and say, Come, let us go up to the mountain of the Lord, to the house of our God of Jacob. He will teach us His ways, and we shall walk in his paths. For out of Zion shall go forth the laws, and the words of the Lord, from Jerusalem." These verses of the scriptures have deceived so many of the faiths. A lot of the faiths in the third world countries have been going up to the top of the mountains praying and fasting for the King to answer prayers. Also, petitions without a considerable number did not have a real understanding of the Proverbs as stated above, that the mountain of the King means the church. Due to the manipulation and cunning of the authorities, they keep quiet over this.

Some of the faiths will be going up to the mountain for prayers with a reference that Jesus, during his wilderness, went up to the mountain and prayed. Thus, if you are among those who go to the mountain for prayers, be advised that the mountain is the house/church of the living King, as we believed. Though mind you, that word is not specific, so how could one reason it: it's all the ways of creating confusion. Again, the scripture says (Isaiah 40:7-8) that "The grass withers, the flowers fade, because the breath of the King blows upon it; surely the people are grassing. The grass withers, the flowers fade, but the words live and abide forever."

My question is, which breath which makes the grass to wither and the flower to fade? Do you know that the beings felt that humans had deceived them? Hoping we had regarded the air which we breathe in and out as his spirits? As a reason, this verse of the scripture is written. However, I'm here to set us free. Men and women are withering until the person dies due to the nature of all living things. And nothing more than that. And the grass fades mostly during the time of winter and dry season, and that is the nature of the world. Which is caused by nobody? Remember how it was explained that the spirits behind the religions even breathe as we do.

I believe we have enough sense to reason correctly. Well, if a king is not properly honoured in his town among his people. What else are we to talk about despite the fact we have discovered the truth? If that is the reason because it's all stories, such a King can't have been raised in a Town/Nation or wherever without proper recognition by his people. Let me ask you, reader, don't you know or recognize your town's King or Queen? I think I do, nevertheless, read on. I will do my best to expose us to revelation before the end of this volume. If the King, as regarded, is not different and has made a decree, at least ninety-eight percent would be subject to that authority as a creator. Right from Jesus' settlement, according to the scripture, very many had rejected him, refused to bow down, and confessed his name as commanded.

Please, give a reason for this; let's assume that God (Spirit) (John 4:24) Say that God is a spirit, had initially created white and black people at the same time. Why then, is it that only a tiny percentage (30/70) of the world population is black, while the rest are white skinned people?

Moreover, why sense, knowledge, technology and even civilization are mostly with the Whites? Also why were the majority of the black countries being colonized by the white people? Adam and Eve, who is black and which one is white the margined are so wide. Only these few points show us that white people must have been in existence; because life is transferable wisdom belongs to the old by virtue of their experienced. Spirit's deception will not last forever.

Here is another excellent point: looking around today at the people/the faiths that believed in him (The Christians) is not even up to thirty per cent of the world population. So, what I'm saying is this; it's time we come out with the truth, if not for any other reason at least for the sake of our coming generation, to lay a good foundation for them. Too many foreigners nationalized in the Western World today where there is a better life without remembering it is a good foundation of their forefathers that brought them today's good living.

So, as we are still living, let's do all we can for the good of our grandchildren. If all was not for deception, that he was a real Jewish offspring, I do not think very many of his people would have rejected him in any way. Scripture says that the devil is a liar.

CONCLUSIONS:

*G*reatest Mistake is a profound book that gives fascinating insights into the spirit world and tells readers about the different types of spirits that exist. Like every other living being, spirits have been in existence for a long time, and there are two types of spirits; the spirit mind and the spirit world. The book will help readers understand how the spirits work because of certain characteristics that make them behave exactly like human beings. The book also reveals how the ancestral spirits have gender and exist as male or female.

The book is a good way to learn about the spirit world and will also make readers understand how the spirits work. The topic is informative and unique and will give readers a glimpse into the spirit world and how they are monitoring people in the world and are always around every one of us. Spirits are capable of doing many things. It is also interesting that spirits cause three-quarters of the problems in humans. The book is an eye-opener to readers on how these spirits can understand the human mind easily, enabling them to gain control over the human mind and body because of the gullibility of human beings. The expression style is simple and fluid, making it easy for readers to understand how spirits soar around humans and, most of the time, influence decisions.

Greatest Mistake plunges the reader into the spirit world and explores the link between the ancestral spirits and humanity. The book explains how the familiar spirits come to be and how they operate. These spirits speak the dialects or the language of the people where they were born, and they have the power to interfere with the human thought process. This means that they can plumb the depths of the human mind and have the power to make people forget things, especially information that is vital to their growth and success. It also explains that these spirits are one of the biggest causes of underdevelopment in Africa.

It also allows my background to speak through the book which is very revealing of a culture where superstition

Conclusions:

intersects with spiritual realities to define the human experience Greatest Mistake is informative, a book that will open the minds of readers to typical African mentality and a spiritual reality that affects our lives deeply.

The book will teach you a lot about your spirituality and what spirits are. Religious in nature, this book is a great source of information for anyone who wants to take the next step in spirituality and find out more about spirits and how they interfere in our lives. As I very clearly explain, there are two different kinds of spirits in this world; some we can see, and some we can interact with, and then there are some that we cannot see, yet they can easily meddle with us. I believe that it is easy to coexist with the spirits if one understands them, and for that, you need all the information you can get to make it work in your favour.

Greatest Mistake is packed with information; the information provided in this book will help you work with the spirits and make them help you; it is still a great read for people who are interested in learning more about spirits and understanding them beyond what the media shares. The narrative is exceptionally well-paced, and the pace is slow enough to help you dig into the subject and be ready for the information provided, it is very interesting and educational book!

Please do yourself more favour; for better digestion of the volumes raised, study part two of the book called Sharp Minded Criminals—best of luck.

Thanks.
Cee Eziamaka.

APOLOGIES

Finally, in any form or shape, anything I have written in this book has offended you, grieved you, or caused inconvenience to you in your marital life, your business, your spiritual life, family life, and even in your societies, I apologise and ask you to please endure because there is no way the truth could be ignored.

Too many people for so long have been in different types of spiritual bondages, mostly religious nations, through the deceptions of the spirit, so in order not to fool ourselves like the ancestors and to keep good records for our children and our great-grandchildren. I consider it vital for humanity that the deception of these spirits is exposed for the freedom, liberation, and growth of the human race.

Many thanks,
Cee Eziamaka

THANKS FOR READING!

Cee Eziamaka

Website: https://greatestmistakesharpmindedcriminals.com/

Email: inforgreatestmistake@gmail.com

www.ingramcontent.com/pod-product-compliance
Lightning Source LLC
Chambersburg PA
CBHW070717160426
43192CB00009B/1226